Praise for *Encounters with Rikki*

"Children who enter the criminal court system as victims may have to relive the abuse they experienced by testifying . . . *Encounters with Rikki* tells the story of an amazing therapy dog who helps children cope with this stress so they can tell their stories and so justice can be served. It's essential reading."
> —Cynthia J. Najdowski, assistant professor, School of Criminal Justice at the University at Albany

"A moving account of how a loving dog and a determined man can make a world of difference in the lives of those who need it most."
> —Janice Gary, author of *Short Leash: A Memoir of Dog Walking and Deliverance*

"A compelling story of the human-animal bond at its absolute finest."
> —Mary R. Burch, PhD, director of the AKC Canine Good Citizen and Therapy Dog Programs

"*Encounters with Rikki* tells the story of a truly amazing bond between man and dog and the life-saving healing and companionship their relationship has inspired . . . [It captures] the magical way in which therapy animals unlock love and trust for those who most desperately need it."

—Lauren Book, MS.Ed, founder and
CEO of Lauren's Kids foundation

"This riveting story will forever change how you view the power of animal therapy."

—Martha Barnett, former president of
the American Bar Association

"An extremely moving book . . . A profoundly human journey told through the unlikely story of a canine."

—Armand B. Cognetta Jr., chief of dermatology,
Florida State University College of Medicine

Encounters with Rikki

Encounters with Rikki

*From Hurricane Katrina Rescue
to Exceptional Therapy Dog*

JULIE STRAUSS BETTINGER

INKSHARES

Published by Inkshares Inc., San Francisco, California
www.inkshares.com

Edited and designed by Girl Friday Productions
www.girlfridayproductions.com
Cover design by John Barnett and Anna Curtis
Cover photo by Dave Barfield

ISBN-13: 9781941758533
eISBN: 9781941758540

Library of Congress Control Number: 2015942734

First edition

Printed in the U.S.A.

This book is dedicated to all the children who have ever given testimony against their sexual abuser and all the court personnel and volunteer animal-assisted therapy teams who work tirelessly to protect them.

TABLE OF CONTENTS

AUTHOR'S NOTE

I offer this cautionary note to readers: the title and theme of this book can be deceptive. It might sound like a "dog story," suggesting light reading, but *Encounters* contains some serious, adult-oriented content related to sex crimes against children. I tried to carefully craft the presentation of these crimes in the story line to convey their gravity yet minimize shock. But it's an emotional subject, and I want the reader to be forewarned.

Writing about victims of sexual abuse requires effort to protect identity, so some names have been changed, and in cases where I was given permission to disclose real names, only the first were used. I am forever grateful to the children and their parents for allowing me the privilege of including their stories.

Find more stories about using therapy dogs in the courtroom to comfort victims and witnesses at EncountersWithRikki.com.

PROLOGUE

CHOICES

A series of urgent questions on a late August weekend in 2005 determined the fate of a quarter of a million pets in America.

Newscasters reported that a tropical depression formed in the Bahamas had ballooned into a hurricane now called Katrina. It cut a swath across South Florida and by Friday morning had arched S-like headed north, strengthened by warm waters in the Gulf of Mexico.

For the third time in six weeks, Louisiana and Mississippi residents had to ask themselves, *Do we go? Do we stay? What are our options?*

Every pet's life depended on how their people answered, from the mama cat and her kittens to the iguana, parakeet, bunnies, boas, three-pound Chihuahuas, and one-hundred-pound Great Danes.

Answers did not come easily. Everyone had to consider finances, available transportation, and dependents, including the size and number of pets in a household. They also took into account their previous experience with hurricanes, along with well-intentioned advice from neighbors or friends. And this information was weighed against the owners' tolerance for risk.

Hurricane fatigue blunted advisories and preparedness messages. Ten times in the last seven years, the homes, businesses, and communities along the Gulf Coast had been in the path of a hurricane. And all, including Cindy and Dennis just six weeks earlier, had been false alarms for their area.

Those who had evacuated previously knew that leaving was not a simple solution. It meant hours-long traffic jams, gas shortages, soaring temperatures, and testy attitudes. Relatives would be inconvenienced; hotels—if you could find one with vacancies—were expensive; and dining out for three meals a day added up. Then, two days later, evacuees would have to fight their way back into the city, only to find it untouched.

So here we go again. *Just another fire drill?*

As the storm warnings increased Saturday and Sunday, many were tempted to take shortcuts or risks. They thought, *I'll pack up, safeguard my animals at home, leave, and be back in two days, just like last time.* Or, *I'll just stay here with my pets.*

Official disaster-planning scenarios at the time did not consider animals; pet owners along the Gulf Coast were on their own. The only instructions related to animal companions were warnings about the lack of accommodations. Red Cross shelters didn't allow pets, and neither did most hotels.

Well-meaning spokespersons advised evacuees to leave their pets behind. Put them in an enclosed area without windows, such as a closet, where they will be safe from flying debris or glass, they said. Animals should be secured so they will not run away when frightened by the howling winds and sheets of rain. And leave enough food and water for three days, when owners will most likely be able to return to their homes.

To many residents that meant caging or crating their pets or confining them to a bathroom or windowless garage. If a dog wasn't used to the indoors, it would be chained outside on a porch, perhaps, the owner believing the animal would be happier that way.

Those who found such suggestions unacceptable put their own lives on the line and remained with their pets. Yes, they would tough it out together.

In the end, the actions of their human caregivers influenced whether pets would survive the storm; if they could be rescued by strangers and transported to a shelter with hundreds of other strays; whether they would suffer injury, starvation, dehydration, or drowning; and whether, in the best of circumstances, they would be reunited with their owners or adopted by a new family. If they lived, the experience would change the pets' personalities forever.

* * *

The day before Katrina made its second landfall, this time near the Louisiana-Mississippi border, the National Oceanic and Atmospheric Administration described the catastrophic damage expected:

> *Most of the area will be uninhabitable for weeks, perhaps longer. Even well-constructed homes will have roof and wall failure. All gabled roofs will fail, leaving those homes severely damaged or destroyed. All wood-framed low-rising apartment buildings will be destroyed. Airborne debris will be widespread and may include heavy items such as appliances and even vehicles. Persons, pets and livestock exposed to the winds will face certain death if struck. Water shortages will make human suffering incredible by modern standards. Livestock exposed to the wind will be killed.*

This time, the predictions were right.

Creatures left in the path of Hurricane Katrina were severely traumatized, injured, or killed. There was no safe place during the twelve hours the winds raged and rain pelted the Gulf Coast or when the thirty-foot wall of water flooded canals in Mississippi and breached levees, submerging New Orleans in toxic sludge.

Katrina claimed the lives of many animal victims within a few hours. Caged inside, they treaded water until their heads reached the top of the crate and they drowned. Chained to trees, their bodies were slung around, hitting walls or fences, their lives finally coming to an end by choking. Left inside, they clawed at doors and chewed through Sheetrock, until the structures crushed them.

Pets that managed to survive were suddenly thrust into a foreign environment. Abandoned and confused, they had no food, water, or human contact. Their keen senses of eyesight, smell, and hearing that helped them interpret the world were of no use in the unfamiliar landscape. Unknown dangers lurked everywhere.

They remained for weeks or months in attics and on rooftops in one-hundred-degree heat. They swam through chemical- and sewage-laden water, which burned their skin. They lay in bathtubs and behind toilets in their own excrement, many times with other pets. Within a few weeks, some would go through a second storm, Hurricane Rita, and lose their fight for survival.

* * *

If you've ever given your heart over to a dog, cat, hamster, or horse, the idea of abandoning them in a hurricane would be unfathomable. But when Katrina hit in August 2005, there were choices to be made and Gulf Coast residents made them. Most waited until warnings accelerated and mandatory evacuation was ordered before responding. They made decisions within a matter of minutes and in the most dire of circumstances. They didn't count on storm surges flooding canals in Mississippi or levees being breached in New Orleans.

Many people did things in the best interest of their animals that still resulted in the loss or death of their pets. Perhaps they stayed, but officials later forced them to abandon their pets to board a rescue craft or enter an emergency shelter. Or they refused rescue efforts and perished along with their animals.

In hindsight, it's easy to judge, to second-guess their choices. Those who didn't experience Katrina personally have so many questions, and there is really only one answer.

"In Katrina, there was nowhere to go with your pets," a Humane Society staffer noted. "There was nowhere to take them. We lost a lot of lives because people wouldn't leave without their pets and a lot of pets' lives because people had no choice *but* to leave them."

After weeks of witnessing scenes where pets had fought for their lives and lost, and coaxing starving, injured, and frightened animals to safety, one pet rescuer said she finally came to the realization that "the pets were left behind to *live*. The owners thought they were protecting them."

Volunteers came from all parts of the United States and even overseas to be boots on the ground for the animals. Touching—and tragic—images continue to be shared on the Internet of what turned into the world's largest animal-rescue operation. One black-and-white Lab mix presses his body against a rescuer's ankle, wrapping his front paw around the man's foot. In another batch of photos, a frighteningly thin dachshund licks the face of her rescuer, and a skin-and-bones cat uses what energy he has left to rub against a volunteer's leg. The clinging of these animals to the humans seems to communicate the same message: "I am finally safe."

A clinical psychologist from New York, who canceled all her appointments and raced to the Gulf Coast, tells about a skeletal little pit bull that she and a friend rescued on a street in the Upper Ninth Ward of New Orleans. "Upon her rescue, she crawled right past the food we put out for her and into my lap. She was starving when we found her but craved human touch and comfort more than the food. She just sat still . . . with her face pressed up against mine for the longest time. It was on a day that we were not supposed to bring animals back to (the emergency shelter) because they were full and would only take criticals. This was critical in our book."

Sweetie, as the pit was later named, became one of the estimated twenty-five thousand animals that were saved. Groups like the Humane Society of the United States' Animal Rescue Team banded together using any means possible to get help for the stranded pets. So-called rogue groups, small bands of people who wanted to help and thought the rules of larger organizations were slowing things down, patched together their own search-and-rescue efforts.

The biggest operation, based at the Lamar Dixon Expo Center in Gonzales, Louisiana—sixty miles north of New Orleans—cared for an estimated 8,500 animals in less than six weeks. A series of operations in Mississippi cared for 1,800 or more. All had the goal of reuniting pets with their original owners, but in the end, only about 23 percent made it. The rest went to foster homes, were adopted out if the owner could not be located, or were surrendered because owners were not in a position to take them back.

"Hurricane Katrina Rescue" became a leading brand name among pet lovers, and animal shelters throughout the US were swamped with calls from people clamoring to adopt. Animal-welfare groups operate on a shoestring budget with nearly all-volunteer staff, so the increase in calls alone was overwhelming. Because most of these organizations have strict guidelines for fostering and adoption, the process of placing pets can be slow. As they received Katrina rescues from emergency shelters in the affected areas, adoption organizers had to consider medical needs—including spaying and neutering—and conduct behavioral assessments before matching pets with an approved home.

At the same time, the shelters were dealing with a great number of evacuee "owner give-ups." People were sleeping with their pets in cars, camping out under blue tarps in Walmart parking lots, and seeking shelter at pet-friendly RV parks, trying their best to avoid giving up their pets.

Tallahassee, Florida, became a haven for Mississippi evacuees, and many without other alternatives bunked in the Red Cross shelter at the Church of Jesus Christ of Latter-Day Saints. This capital city of Florida, an hour north of the Gulf and somewhat insulated from major storm fury, had received a lot of practice sheltering in two years of unusually high hurricane activity. The previous summer, organizers had made arrangements for people to stay with their pets at a local high school. But Katrina hit during the school year, and there was a lack of other facilities that could accommodate both humans and animals, so local veterinarians and kennels offered free boarding. Some hotels also loosened their standards to allow guests to keep their pets with them.

For those with one or two dogs or cats, the arrangements were satisfactory, but those with very large or very young pets—like the family with eight Great Danes, including one that was pregnant—were on their own.

As people who had evacuated with their pets received word about the level of devastation and destruction, they went into survival mode. Many showed up at Humane Society offices and city shelters—their dog on a leash or their cat crated—and surrendered them. They didn't know what they were returning to or where they would be living in the near future and told animal-welfare staff they felt better knowing their pet was safe in someone else's home.

Ten days after the hurricane, Tallahassee's animal shelter had 521 dogs, cats, and "various other critters" in a facility designed to house 350 animals. The shelter was usually at capacity that time of year, further compounding the problem. Unable to accommodate more strays, they started farming animals out to a hundred foster families. The shelter put out an SOS in the community, looking for people with fenced yards who could temporarily foster the Katrina pets.

Four weeks post-Katrina, as animal-rescue groups continued battling the elements and risking their lives to save pets left behind, calls to the Leon County Humane Society in Tallahassee had increased to about fifty a day, mostly people wanting a "Katrina pet." Concerned citizens also offered to donate food, supplies, or money, while evacuees asked about referrals to a vet, free dog food, and any services the society could spare.

One Katrina evacuee was at her wits' end. She had lost her home and workplace in Mississippi and could no longer care for her golden retriever and its two thirteen-week-old puppies. With no Red Cross emergency shelters that could accommodate such a foursome—and certainly no hotel—she had been securing lodging any way possible. Trying to manage the energy levels of puppies—keeping them confined so they didn't destroy their temporary living quarters—and perhaps to get donated dog food and supplies, plus the uncertainty about her future, drove the choice: she could no longer protect them.

She had to leave them behind—to *live*.

CHAPTER 1

MAKING IT

In the late afternoon of September 26, 2005, in a kennel-scented office, volunteers cradled two golden retriever puppies for the Humane Society's version of a jail-booking photo. The one with a red collar peered directly into the camera, and her handler used a firm hold to keep her in place. The other looked despondent; she offered a reluctant mug, bracing herself against the volunteer's arm with her front paw.

The phone was ringing nonstop, as a handful of volunteers and staff members tried to field questions, mostly about Hurricane Katrina pets. Melissa Abernathy, the resident "dog person," had to get these latest arrivals into a foster home before closing time, as their operation was not equipped for boarding. The thirteen-week-old puppies could be separated from their mom, who was also surrendered, but Melissa wanted to keep the puppies together as playmates. They are more easily managed that way.

She looked at her list of foster homes. All booked. Overbooked, really. She was going to have to make some exceptions to the rules. After a few calls, she convinced a former board member, who was not on her foster list but loved golden retrievers, to take the puppies for a few days. That would buy some time until she had a longer-range plan.

Piles of paper littered Melissa's desk, many of them owner give-up sheets that accompany new arrivals. At surrender, owners fill out a form that serves as a combination thumbprint and rap sheet: *What breed or mix? Spayed/neutered? Approximate age? Has this dog bitten anyone? What is this dog's reaction to cats? To other dogs? How about visitors?*

Some questions can be emotionally difficult for owners to answer: *Which best describes your dog (cuddly, playful, independent, loyal)? What is your dog's favorite type of toy?* And the one buried at the bottom of the sheet: *Please circle any that apply to explain why you have surrendered this dog.* Among the owner's choices: *I am allergic. This pet has behavior issues I can't manage. I don't have time to care for this pet.* A line next to the choice *other* left room for cases like the two goldens: *We are victims of Hurricane Katrina.*

* * *

In this North Florida town, the ninety-degree heat and news of destruction just a few hours west were stifling the community's transition into fall. Local headlines that would normally be celebrating Florida State University football coach Bobby Bowden's thirtieth year and third victory of the season were crowded out by Katrina:

> *Hundreds dead or missing in Mississippi*
> *New Orleans slowly drowns*
> *"This is our tsunami"*

Dramatic images accompanied the stories: an apartment building with its interior walls dangling from balconies, a grimacing teenager who couldn't find her family, a woman sharing bottled water with a dog as a human corpse floated in the murky river below.

Evidence of the devastation was difficult to ignore. A shopping center hosted a giveaway for refugees to obtain vital services. Restaurants, therapists, and a truck from Walmart packed the place. One volunteer said, "We gave away T-shirts, and they were so thankful. For people who had nothing, a T-shirt was a pretty big deal."

At their home in a dense forest on the outskirts of Tallahassee, Chuck and Patty Mitchell were discussing their next move to help hurricane efforts. Patty had already sent a check to the Red Cross. She also called the local animal shelter to have their names added to a list for fostering, since they had a fenced backyard and a friendly Labrador retriever. Over the roar of barking dogs, a voice said someone would get back to her.

Patty was at her dentist's office the following week and met a woman in the parking lot. She was giving water to three dogs, so Patty walked over to pet them. She remarked on how well groomed they were. The woman, who looked to be in her midthirties, thanked her. She said two of them belonged to her and her boyfriend, who was inside getting a root canal. The third was a Katrina rescue. They had found him on the road while evacuating. "We figured it's what we needed to do."

Patty called her husband soon after her appointment. "We are losers," she told Chuck. "We've got to call the animal shelter again." This time they were referred to the Humane Society. After talking it over, they decided to call their friend Pam Houmere instead.

Pam and her husband, Bill Armstrong, both in their early fifties, were like the prom king and queen of rescuers. Their home had served as a stop-off for more than a thousand animals, including horses, since 1980. Certainly, they would know how the Mitchells could help.

"You're in luck," Pam told Patty. "Can you foster two golden retriever puppies?"

Pam and Bill generally didn't foster puppies, but the Humane Society needed to move two goldens from a board member's home—they had destroyed a rug—so they partitioned part of their kitchen for the pups. After nearly a week Pam and Bill had started calling the lively one "Diana," a name that means "heavenly" in Roman mythology, and her sister "Aphrodite," after the Greek goddess of love and beauty.

Pam told Patty the dogs would require crates, frequent potty breaks, house training, and constant effort to prevent destruction because of their irresistible urge to chew. The Mitchells said yes, they'd take them.

Chuck and Patty's home is nestled in five acres of woods at the foot of a swamp where it's not unusual to hear the guttural growl of a gator. Chuck occasionally has to dismantle beaver dams that divert the creek, flooding yards and homes. He built the house himself with the help of neighbors while living in a tent on the property in the 1970s. Fresh out of college, he passed on a fellowship at Yale to study utopian communities and started one instead. Chuck and a handful of like-minded people named it the Miccosukee Land Co-op. With his first dog, Gabrielle, he cut all the roads of the intentional community with a machete.

The intentional project unintentionally launched his career as a homebuilder. Along the way, he met Patty, who liked, among other things, that Chuck wasn't interested in having children and was "man enough to have his dog neutered." They married in 1983.

In Chuck and Patty's fenced backyard, Roscoe the happy Lab sat and watched expectantly as the fourteen-pound puppies were carried in. Pam and Bill set the dogs on the grass, and Diana immediately ran toward Roscoe, who was easily five times her size, wiggling her body and jumping up to lick his muzzle. Her littermate, Aphrodite, sniffed the ground a bit, then sat and watched her sibling, seemingly content with the show.

Pam said the one with the red collar, Diana, was scheduled to go to a permanent home, but Aphrodite would need longer care if the Mitchells were willing. Chuck and Patty said they would consider it.

Over the next few days, Diana was normal, healthy, and full of spunk, while Aphrodite was sickly and sluggish. Chuck and Patty guessed it might be the change of food or environment, or some leftover hurricane-related trauma. She had difficulty eating and occasionally vomited. Dogs will rarely mess in their crate, but she did. And she was intensely frightened of rain and loud noises. Roscoe was smitten with Diana, while Aphrodite passively observed them play.

So this little one needs a home, and Roscoe could use a playmate, Chuck thought. Maybe it was time to add to their family. The more sober in their partnership, Patty reminded her husband that Aphrodite was going to need some rehabilitation. And Patty would be leaving for a trip to California with her sister in a few weeks. Would Chuck be able to manage alone? "Well," he joked, "we could always switch their collars—do you think anyone would notice?"

Chuck sat on the steps overlooking the fenced yard and the three dogs. He felt the weight of those images: hurricane refugees, helpless starving animals, and displaced families—real homelessness. And there was no telling how many temporary shelters this puppy had already been in during her young life. She needed a forever home.

He told Patty, "Roscoe and I will take care of this dog while you're away. Aphrodite can stay." To make it official, they gave her a new name: Rikki Lake Pontchartrain Mitchell.

A rescued pet's history is often reflected in its behavior and habits. If a dog was traumatized at the hands of a male handler, she might be skittish around men. Some are frightened of trucks, having received injuries after being ejected from one, and many just have difficulty trusting humans, the result of any kind of drama in their young lives. Whatever their experience, it becomes a permanent imprint on the swirls of their personality. So the week Patty was gone, Chuck spent as much time as possible with Rikki in an effort to build trust and start to instill confidence in her that she would not be abandoned again.

Every waking moment that he wasn't with Rikki, he was negotiating the sale of a company that manufactured gate operators, which he'd rescued from bankruptcy. It had recovered and was returning a substantial profit, so it was on the auction block. GTO (Gates That Open) had made the list of the fastest-growing small businesses in the United States, and the story of its survival—and Chuck's unconventional management style—had propelled him to the cover of *Inc.* magazine. Twice.

The board of directors, whom Chuck had recruited as investors in the company, had convinced him to take over after the founder had suffered a heart attack while horseback riding and died. Chuck took leave from his construction company and rolled up his sleeves. Instead of cutting jobs and slashing budgets—the textbook approach to averting financial ruin—he started making small changes to transform the company's culture. He insisted that the board set aside 5 percent of the earnings in a profit-sharing plan for employees, then personally guaranteed a substantial line of credit. Chuck also introduced flexible work schedules, raised employees' pay, and gave them better health insurance. He reasoned that making people comfortable frees them to come up with ideas for making the business better. Additionally, Chuck improved coffee service, patched the roof, and encouraged employees to use the company's tools to repair their personal automobiles after hours. It was a 180-degree change from their previous boss, who was known for managing by intimidation. Chuck's way of thinking was to "tap the inner reserves" of the team. When employees received the much-promised profit share at the end of the year—checks folded inside a gift bag with a T-shirt—some of them cried. A significant recovery followed.

As major shareholders of the company, Chuck and Patty would have a different life if the sale went through. They would have a nice monetary cushion, and the company's employees, profit, and future would no longer dominate Chuck's thoughts. He and Patty had always said they wanted to work until retirement, then work for free through community service—Chuck just never imagined it happening at fifty-three.

With Rikki's special needs, Chuck made the thirty-minute trip between his office and home several times a day to give her a potty break and clean up any mess she'd made. Strangely, he didn't feel inconvenienced. When he returned to the office after taking care of Rikki, he had a different attitude. Chuck had been around dogs all his life, but things were different with Rikki. He couldn't explain it; he just knew.

After a few weeks, Rikki's health stabilized, and she settled in as the newest member of the family, becoming more adventurous in the yard alongside her new big brother, Roscoe. She often deferred to him, barking encouragement as the Lab dug holes and threw dirt in her face. More diva than clown, Rikki wasn't the party girl like many others in her breed. Her dark-brown soulful eyes created a look that was just this side of worried. In contrast to Roscoe and other dogs they'd owned, Rikki seemed to prefer Chuck and Patty's company over that of her own kind. In turn they found her surprisingly affectionate, wise, and pensive.

Rikki also invited physical interaction. She didn't mind having her nails clipped, while Roscoe resisted any attempt to touch his paws. Even as she grew, Rikki clambered up into Chuck's lap as if she were Yorkie size. One day, Chuck walked into the living room to find Patty napping on the couch, a nearly full-grown Rikki lying across her like a blanket, her head snuggled up to Patty's cheek.

Something else was different about her. Rikki visually engaged anyone she met. When she looked at Chuck, he felt as if she could see inside of him and know what he was feeling.

With Roscoe graduating from basic dog obedience, they enrolled Rikki, and Chuck took over the leash to assure consistency in training. At their first meeting, veteran dog trainer Jay King knew there was something different about the reddish golden. He had trained more than a thousand dogs and handlers, and he told Chuck that Rikki was special. She was shy around the other dogs, so Jay encouraged Chuck to listen to his dog, to give her room to be who she wanted to be. "Look for behaviors you want and reward them; ignore those you don't want."

One session, Jay noticed Rikki leading Chuck across the room. A twelve-year-old girl helping to train the family dog, Snickers, was nervous and getting confused about the commands. Rikki moved right up to the girl, with Chuck trailing her, and dropped her head slightly as if asking permission to come closer. The little girl responded by reaching out to pet Rikki, and Chuck and Jay both noticed her smile and relax. The child was more confident during the balance of the session. "Chuck, you've got a good dog here," Jay told him. "That's an angel in a dog's body."

A few weeks later, Chuck was walking in their rural community while Rikki explored off leash. As they approached a neighborhood woman who is unsteady from the effects of Parkinson's, she called out and asked Chuck to leash his dog. As they came closer, Rikki's disposition changed; she bowed her head, then reached her nose out tentatively to the woman as they met. It was as though the dog knew this human was delicate.

Chuck described Rikki's behavior to her veterinarian at the next checkup. Dr. Julia Stege said she, too, noticed something special about Rikki. "Dogs will read people's body language," she told Chuck, and many times that puts the dogs in a defensive mode. But Rikki seemed to respond with empathy. It wasn't a breed-specific temperament, either, and definitely couldn't be taught. Dr. Stege said she reads a dog during visits and pays attention to their level of arousal. Unlike most other dogs, Rikki engaged her visually and welcomed her examinations. She reached out and stroked the golden's long red coat, and Rikki met her gaze. "She's a sweetheart. She would never harm anyone."

Dr. Stege mentioned that her clinic was screening dogs for an animal therapy program and told Chuck that nine-month-old Rikki might be a good fit. The local group trained teams of humans and their companion pets (dogs and cats, mostly) to visit with patients in hospitals, rehab centers, a hospice house, and nursing homes. With Chuck's people skills, she thought they would make a good team. She gave him the organization's phone number.

That evening, Chuck started researching the science behind animal therapy. Animals have been used therapeutically since the ninth century in Belgium. Even Sigmund Freud believed that dogs had a special sense that allowed them to judge a person's character accurately. Freud's favorite chow chow, Jofi, attended all of his therapy sessions.

The American Veterinary Medical Association officially recognized the human-animal bond in 1982 due in part to hundreds of clinical trials that confirmed what people had known for thousands of years: petting an animal significantly reduces stress and anxiety.

Chuck found studies that proved pets actually caused a chemical reaction in humans. When a person interacts with a therapy animal, there is a dramatic, measurable decrease in heart rate and blood pressure. The amount of cortisol, a stress-inducing hormone, is reduced in the bloodstream, too. And petting a dog or cat for as little as a minute stimulates the production of oxytocin—the same hormone that enhances trust, cooperation, and love between a parent and a child. Petting a therapy animal also releases endorphins, making people feel better by diminishing feelings of pain, depression, and loneliness.

All of the studies noted that not every dog is well suited for the job of therapy animal and that the handler's temperament could also make or break the team. Chuck looked over at Rikki sprawled out on the couch, asleep. He was pretty sure their little gift from Katrina had what it takes, even if he wasn't as confident about himself.

* * *

With his six-foot-five-inch frame, Chuck was hard to miss when he walked into the community service center for the initial animal therapy evaluation. Charismatic and grinning like a Labrador puppy himself, he emanated enthusiasm. Program Director Stephanie Perkins liked Chuck's devotion to his dog, and Rikki impressed her by breezing through the screening, obeying all commands and demonstrating her friendliness toward strangers. The two were invited to the weekly meetings to build on those skills. Stephanie told Chuck that Rikki needed to learn how to interact safely and reliably with the elderly and impaired, including being exposed to equipment used in the medical facilities, such as wheelchairs and walkers. This was done through role-playing with volunteers exhibiting behaviors typical for visits.

Chuck and Rikki arrived at a recreation center where teams of dogs and handlers met for the first class. They walked down a hallway and into an open room with chairs arranged theater-style. As they approached the crowd, two-year-old Rikki, smaller than the average golden retriever, began panting. Her gait was stiff and her tail was taut. A dozen or so people were greeting each other and getting tangled in leashes as the dogs traded friendly hellos, but Rikki was leaning into Chuck's leg. About half the dogs were full-sized goldens, probably eighty pounds to Rikki's fifty.

One of the more overeager ones strained his leash toward Rikki, who returned the greeting with a low growl. Knowing that his petite, passive girl didn't warm up to strange dogs quickly, Chuck moved to take a seat and try to settle her down. Within minutes, though, Rikki snarled at another golden, and Chuck could see her body language was snarling, too.

From the front of the room, Stephanie called for everyone's attention. "Okay, we're going to go ahead and get started." She introduced herself and welcomed the teams. She explained that during the training there would be people in the group without pets who would be used in role-playing. They had specific purposes—some would be loud, others would simulate a person's lack of motor skills, another would be in a wheelchair. The actors represented a range of ages—little kids, teenagers, and seniors. The idea was for the dogs to be exposed to a variety of people and situations so their human partners could see how they react.

"I'll break you up into groups, and we'll take turns allowing your dog to interact with the role players."

As hard as he was trying to pay attention, Chuck kept noticing that his previously passive dog continued to scowl at her canine counterparts. If one even inched toward her, she showed her teeth. Chuck corrected her quietly: "*Rikki.*" She looked up apologetically, but when another dog got close, her upper lip retracted again.

Chuck started looking for an opening to rescue his dog (and himself) from the increasingly volatile situation. As Stephanie paused and referred to some notes, Chuck rose and headed for the door. But his Clydesdale size didn't make for a discreet departure. Stephanie's eyes were following him; she turned and told the group, "Hold on—I'll be right back," and caught up to Chuck in the hallway.

"Where are you going?"

"I'm sorry," he said, turning toward her, "but this isn't for us. It's just not going to work. Rikki doesn't like other dogs, I guess. So I don't think she's ever going to make it as a therapy dog."

"You don't have to leave," Stephanie insisted. "You can just move her farther away. Give her more space at the back of the room so she doesn't feel threatened or uncomfortable around the other dogs."

It wasn't about how Rikki got along with other dogs anyway. It was how she got along with people. Rikki enjoyed being touched by strangers, and she was super sweet. Stephanie could tell Chuck was going to be a good team member, too.

"The back of the class, huh?" Chuck laughed. "Well, that's where I spent most of my high school days."

It was a save that Stephanie would recall many times over the next few years—the story about how one of their best therapy teams almost got away.

CHAPTER 2

TRUTH SERUM

Midafternoon on a late winter day, a petite golden retriever appeared at the employee entrance of the Leon County Courthouse. Freshly bathed and brushed, Rikki Lake Pontchartrain Mitchell stepped inside the sliding glass doors and swished her tail in gentle greeting at the uniformed deputies. Following two steps behind her, in his own uniform of a white polo tucked into baggy khakis, was her owner, a tall man with a thick head of metallic-silver hair. He said hello to the men and hoisted his knap-sack onto the X-ray conveyor belt. If the deputy found anything peculiar in its contents—two water bottles, a dog brush, a bowl, poop bags, hand-sanitizing gel, and a Ziploc of organic baby carrots—he refrained from comment.

Chuck moved the leash slightly, motioning for Rikki to step through the metal detector. When the alarm sounded, the dog halted so the deputy with a wand could confirm that her metal ID and rabies tags were the culprit. Both officers kept their eyes on Rikki, and Chuck felt himself disappear. He watched as the dog's brow furrowed and she seemed to read their disposition. Her head dropped slightly, as if seeking permission, before she moved closer to claim her reward: one deputy's hand on her head and the other deputy stroking her back.

Rikki's workday had begun.

* * *

Chuck considered these types of encounters while serving as an animal therapy team a bonus. Rikki's primary mission for the day was waiting upstairs, in the form of a child victim who was about to have her first experience of the legal system in Florida. By law, this seven-year-old girl was required to give details about the most horrific thing that she'd ever experienced. She had to tell her story to a defense attorney—whose job was to discredit her—in a formal hearing, facing the man who committed the crime, and again in front of the same man and a nine-member jury of strangers, while sitting in an adult-sized witness chair with a black-robed judge enthroned above.

As a courthouse therapy dog, it was Rikki's job to get the child ready.

Susan Parmalee, the child's victim advocate, met Chuck and Rikki in the marbled rotunda upstairs. A picture of softness with bangs, chestnut hair, and a flowing skirt, she greeted Chuck with a side hug and stroked the top of Rikki's head. Susan wasn't a dog person—she preferred cats—but she had fallen under the influence of Rikki's charm and now had a collection of miniature retriever figurines lining her bookshelves.

The mother and child were waiting upstairs in Susan's office, she said, but Chuck and Rikki would need to use the employee elevator, since therapy dogs were not allowed to use the public ones. Rikki trotted to stay in step with their exercise-walk pace toward the south lobby. She managed to get a quick sniff of a planter but otherwise restrained her natural instincts that weren't part of today's job description. Rikki paused at the elevators, and when the doors opened, she moved easily over the threshold without alarm. She turned to face the opening like the two-legged creatures around her.

Susan gave Chuck a few more details on the case. A defense attorney planned to take the first grader's deposition later that week. Zoe was about five years old when the sexual abuse occurred, and the case had stalled for two years. The child had not talked about it since her videotaped forensics interview forty-eight hours after the incident, so they didn't know if she could recall the facts or would be willing to revisit the memory. Susan and Prosecutor John Hutchins, who was trying the case for the state, hoped having Rikki around would lessen the girl's anxiety, increase her focus, and reduce the chance of further traumatization. Zoe's mother, who would also be called as a witness, had remained patient in spite of the continuous delays by the court. The case involved a close family friend, but Danielle wanted justice. She liked the idea of a volunteer therapy dog team and thought her daughter would be receptive, even though their family didn't have pets.

As soon as Chuck and Rikki rounded the corner near Susan's office, Zoe abandoned the kids' toy collection and came running to the dog. Her tiny hands discovered Rikki's soft velvety ears, and Zoe's blue eyes looked up at the giant man at the end of the leash. She wanted to know everything about her new friend—what is her name? How old is she? Where does she live?

Chuck lowered himself to the child's level and held a baby carrot in front of Rikki, which she delicately received. Zoe's eyes grew wide. "Can I feed her one, too?"

Chuck told Zoe that Rikki was a very special dog. When she was only nine weeks old, she and her sister and mom lost their home during Hurricane Katrina. They were brought to Tallahassee, and Rikki found her forever home with Chuck and his wife, Patty. The dog was now four years old.

"Do you want to see one of her tricks?" Zoe nodded eagerly. He held a baby carrot in front of Rikki's nose and said, "Kiss," then put the carrot between his lips. Rikki's nose approached his face slowly and she parted her teeth, gently retrieving the carrot. Zoe's face lit up. "Can I try?" Chuck looked toward her mom, who nodded, so he handed the girl a carrot.

After a few attempts, Zoe mastered the trick. Chuck told her how Rikki loved to chase squirrels, that she had a brother named Roscoe, a yellow Lab, at home, and that Rikki especially liked to be scratched behind her ears. Zoe promptly reached out and started stroking behind one ear; the dog's head leaned into her doll-sized hand, and Chuck saw Rikki's jaw relax in contentment, as if she were smiling.

About fifteen minutes into the visit, Zoe lay on the floor next to Rikki, an arm draped over the dog's belly. Rikki was lying on her side, perfectly still, her long red lashes only partly closed, as she remained alert to her surroundings. Chuck was sitting on the floor, still holding the leash but giving them space, and Danielle sat in a chair against the wall. All watched the scene unfold like a movie.

Prosecuting Attorney John Hutchins appeared at the door and stopped when he saw the dog and child. Susan Parmalee knelt down next to Rikki, stroked her fur, and asked Zoe if she remembered what happened that time between her and Mr. Frank. Quietly, the girl answered, "Yes."

Did she think she could tell Rikki about it?

Zoe turned her face toward the dog's head and began, story-like, recalling what happened that Saturday night when her mother had put her and her brother, Eli, to bed. The family had been suffering from the flu that week, and the refrigerator was bare. Zoe's parents called their best friends to see if one of them could stay at the house while they went to Walmart. Ms. Heather couldn't make it, but Mr. Frank said he was happy to help out.

Zoe rubbed the dog's ears as she whispered the story. During some parts, she gazed off in the distance, and during others, she propped herself up on an elbow to look into Rikki's eyes as if to make her understand. When Zoe's attention and the story faded, it was obvious to everyone in the room: Rikki's gift had worked; they would have a stronger witness because of her.

CHAPTER 3

RESCUE TO THE RESCUE

Before courthouse therapy dogs like Rikki, there were playing cards—endless games of go fish and old maid. Victim advocates use crayons, coloring books, and a corner bookshelf stacked with purple ponies, red fire engines, and various stuffed critters to help children forget why they're there.

Forgetting is how most kids cope when they are victims of violence, sexual or otherwise. Yet remembering is what justice requires.

When a crime involving a child is suspected, police investigators will interview the adults as part of their evidence-gathering procedure but not children. That is left to specialists. Within twenty-four hours a child victim must be taken to a sexual assault nurse examiner (SANE), who collects DNA samples for a rape kit. Think gynecology exams for preschoolers. Within seventy-two hours of the crime, the victim must visit the same facility for a forensics interview, during which a trained social services specialist uses age-appropriate toys to get the child to talk about what happened. Depending on the child's verbal level, the interviewer may use diagrams of a boy and a girl, the kind you see in a pediatrician's office, and ask the child to identify body parts that were involved. The SANE evidence, forensics video, and interview narrative become part of the case file: evidence for law enforcement to make formal charges and arrest suspects, and later for the judge and jury to determine if the charges fit the crime.

In between the origination of a case and its final resolution, there are depositions to take, plea bargains to consider, and case law to review. It could take two years or more before the case goes to trial. Meanwhile the child's life goes on. And she tries her best to forget.

In crimes against children, there is often only one witness—the victim. His or her story is the basis for bringing charges. The child must recall facts of the crime in a deposition—under intense questioning by a defense attorney—in courtroom hearings to determine any number of things, including the victim's credibility. And if there's no last-minute plea, again during a trial with judge and jury.

Like most victim advocates serving the courts, Susan Parmalee works to smooth out some of the rough edges of the process. The advocate serves as a liaison between witnesses and all the court personnel during the numerous stops along the way. She may pair victims and their family members with services such as mental health counseling, support groups, or even monetary compensation. Perhaps most importantly, she prepares the victim for the mental acrobatics ahead—difficult enough for adult victims, far harder for a child.

When children are asked to give embarrassing details, their voices become a whisper, and they will often shield their eyes. They can't look at a person when they talk about what happened. So Parmalee and other victim advocates look for comfort items to give the children something else to focus on.

* * *

Crimes against children have a common theme—broken trust. Very often the child is related to the individual, or the person is an authority figure in their life. It's the ultimate betrayal.

This broken trust with an adult can hinder the work of the very adults seeking to bring justice, and, ideally, to prevent future victims. What Parmalee had learned was that if children can bond with someone in the court system—like the victim advocate, if they have a relationship of trust and a rapport—they are better able to develop that same trust with the prosecutor. And it is up to the prosecutor to coax the story out of them in front of a judge and maybe even a jury.

Court Administrator Susan Wilson, who was responsible for scheduling hearings and trials for the Second Judicial Circuit in Florida, talked about developing trust and other child-related issues numerous times with victim advocates. Wilson had been serving on an animal therapy team with her miniature schnauzer, Lacey, for more than a year, mostly visiting nursing homes. She read an article about therapy dogs being used in a Central Florida courthouse to comfort kids when they had to give testimony at a criminal trial and wondered if the same idea could work for their court.

To Wilson, it made perfect sense. The bond between children and animals is indisputable. Even if a child doesn't grow up with a dog, cat, or other companion animal, they are surrounded by images of animals on wallpaper, pajama tops, and toothbrush handles. They know that Clifford is a big red dog and at their earliest ages can identify Big Bird, Nemo, and Winnie-the-Pooh. Their expectation of animals, unless they've had a bad experience with one, is pure.

Studies backed up the concept, too. After only five minutes of contact with an unfamiliar dog, 76 percent of children between the ages of seven and fifteen believed that the dog knew how they felt. Another 84 percent indicated they would confide secrets to a dog.

Child advocacy centers (CACs) in some states use therapy animals for SANE medical exams, forensics interviews, and in counseling sessions. Pookie, a nine-pound Siamese cat with pink ears and marine-blue eyes, formed a special bond with a ten-year-old boy at a CAC in Jackson, Mississippi. The boy, who had been sexually assaulted by a neighbor, drew a picture of a boxing ring. A stick figure in one corner bore the boy's name, and another figure across the ring identified his assailant. Pookie the cat was also in the picture—he was biting the assailant's head off. A dialogue bubble over the child's likeness read "No!" while over the assailant's figure was the word "Help!"

After learning more about the use of therapy animals, Wilson contacted Victim/Witness Assistance Program director Helene Potlock. She said she had also read the article about the Central Florida court and she'd had the same idea, so they discussed the next step: getting the chief judge—"not a dog guy"—to allow therapy dog teams into the courthouse in order to test the concept. Surprisingly, he said yes. More than a year later, they cleared the final hurdles, including convincing facilities managers that these dogs were "potty trained" and working through liability issues.

Next were the skeptics: prosecuting attorneys, public defenders, and judges.

There's a very small subset of society whose members work in the field of child sexual violence. Most people are insulated from it. It's a carefully crafted world of confidentiality and protocols, procedures and paperwork. So here were Wilson and Potlock, proposing sending volunteers *with dogs* into some of the most precarious relationships in the court.

Not to be deterred, Wilson developed protocols and oaths of confidentiality for volunteers to sign. She worked with the organization that registered therapy dog teams to develop additional training for ones that might be a good fit for the courts. Finally, in August 2007, they were ready to handle their first case. Mickey, a golden retriever, was introduced to an eleven-year-old girl the day of her trial.

According to Potlock, this can be the most difficult time for child witnesses. They don't sleep well the night before, they wake up with butterflies in their stomach, they can't eat. The victim advocate hoped the therapy dog would provide a calm, soothing distraction so the child would not be paralyzed by fear. Curious about the first visit, Potlock made a point to stop by the victim advocate's office where the child and dog were meeting. She saw the girl on the floor next to Mickey, but there was a bonus. The child's mother was on the floor with the dog, too.

* * *

Chuck and Rikki were one of the first teams recruited into the courthouse therapy dog program. In the early days of their training, Chuck requested to serve facilities that most interested him, including a residential setting for people with cerebral palsy and an art day care for developmentally disabled adults. But within the first few minutes of each visit, Rikki showed signs of stress—panting heavily and steering Chuck toward the exit. Chuck again wondered if they would ever make it as a therapy team. Advised by another volunteer to listen to his dog, Chuck paid closer attention to the setting and Rikki's response. He also visited those same facilities with Roscoe, who responded well to the noise, attention, and stimulation. Finally, Chuck understood what Rikki was trying to tell him: because of her passiveness, she had a very different calling. She seemed much more at home in the hospital rehab and pediatric specialty environments. He thought the courthouse would be a good fit as well.

To help victim advocates introduce the therapy dog program to children and their parents, Stephanie Perkins, coordinator of the Tallahassee Memorial Animal Therapy Program, created a three-ring binder with pet therapy team profiles. The cover has headshots of ten of the dogs profiled, from Kiki the Chihuahua to a one-hundred-pound bullmastiff named Gus. It is presented in storybook fashion, with kid-friendly pictures of the canines and their human partners.

One profile reads "Hi, my name is Grendel. I weigh 180 pounds. Lots of people tell me that I'm the biggest dog they've ever seen. . . . Mommy and Daddy picked me up when I was nine weeks old and I already weighed

30 pounds. I'm a real goofball who loves everyone and everything! I look forward to spending some time with you. Love, Grendel."

There's also a spread on a red miniature dachshund named Honey Girl: "I am quiet and gentle, and I love to sit in someone's lap and give them doggie kisses." On another page, Honey Girl introduces her human partner: "This is my Mom, Bobbie Jo. Mom and I have been a therapy team since May 2007. . . . We visit at hospitals, courts . . . [and] at schools to help children learn to read. At any given time I have lots of brothers and sisters because my mom helps with Dachshund Rescue and we foster Dachshunds until they find their 'furever' homes."

Potlock said that just seeing the photos of the dogs seemed to have a calming effect on kids and allowed them to build quick rapport and trust. Without the children's trust, the advocate wouldn't be able to help them in their most vulnerable moments.

In Rikki's profile picture, she's wearing a blue bandana that contrasts with her reddish-golden fur. Her story appears next to the photo: "My home was destroyed during Hurricane Katrina in August, 2005. I was only two months old and very scared. Then I got a new home with my daddy and mommy, and I'm no longer scared.

"I love to go on visits with my daddy and comfort and cuddle with children and their friends. We visit hospitals and help kids in the courts. I even make visits with my mommy to schools to help kids read. If I visit you, maybe you can brush me and rub my belly; I really like that. I will always listen to you, and love playing with you, especially if you feed me a carrot!"

CHAPTER 4

DEPO DOG

Chuck Mitchell's giant form was folded under the conference room table. A pocket in his khaki slacks bulged with organic baby carrots; one hand had a leash wrapped around it, and the other was stroking Rikki's back.

Seated above them, seven-year-old Zoe was occupied with Rikki's head; she alternated between stroking behind her ears and rearranging the fur on her crown. The closet-size deposition room was crowded with suits and ties—two defense attorneys, John Hutchins, Susan Parmalee, and a court reporter. Zoe's mom, Danielle, had moved to a chair in the far corner of the room.

Zoe's case had all the elements of a prosecuting attorney's nightmare: a child must testify, the incident happened at an early verbal stage, and there had been a long delay between the alleged abuse and the trial. Although John Hutchins was skeptical about using therapy dogs initially, after witnessing the encounter between Rikki and Zoe, he was now optimistic that it might help in her case. They would soon know, as Zoe was about to experience her first interrogation by a defense attorney.

* * *

In the eyes of the court, there was more riding on this trial than a verdict alone. Zoe's case would be groundbreaking: it was the first time an animal therapy team had ever been used in a Florida deposition. It was one thing to have them visit in a victim advocate's office, but inviting them into the formal process was an entirely different matter. State law granted children permission to have a "comfort" item with them during depositions, hearings, and trial. These were usually teddy bears, blankets, or a special toy that the court hoped would reduce their anxiety so they could give stronger testimony. But to have a volunteer animal therapy team attend a deposition raised new questions—*Would the dog be too distracting? Could the human handler control it? What about the close quarters?* These depo rooms could be claustrophobic.

It was all new territory for the state attorney's office, which had to balance the needs of the victim with the confines of the court.

That's not all that was new in *State of Florida v. Frank Dieter*. The case had just landed on Defense Attorney Joel Remland's desk a few months before depositions were scheduled. Defendant Dieter was originally assigned a public defender, then retained a private attorney, whom he fired. He was assigned two other public defenders before Remland. All of which created delays in the process. And unfortunately for the defense, a second victim of Dieter's was identified about the same time Remland took over. Now the court would also need to determine whether there were enough similarities to combine the cases, or if they had to be tried separately, further delaying resolution.

The charges against Remland's client were ominous— if found guilty, he was facing two mandatory life sentences. There had been a plea offer on Zoe's case before Remland inherited it: thirty years followed by lifetime probation. But to thirty-six-year-old Dieter, thirty years *seemed like* a life sentence. He pressed Remland to do his thing: discredit expert witnesses, get evidence thrown out, declare a mistrial. Anything to make this nightmare go away.

Prosecutor John Hutchins had only been assigned to the case twelve days longer than Remland. The assistant state attorney handling it previously had been elected circuit court judge, so the tattered and war-weary file found its way to Hutchins shortly after he was reassigned from a neighboring rural county.

For Hutchins, the stakes were also high. He would be responsible for getting a child molester with multiple victims off the street and helping to protect other children from being abused. But he had to balance this with the responsibility of preventing further harm to the ones who had already been violated.

Saving a child from having to relive her nightmare through questions about the sexual assault at deposition or trial is the court's preference. Defense attorneys often use this in their favor to win support during plea negotiations, "so the child doesn't have to testify." This statement suggests that the prosecuting attorney can protect his client from being tested for competency in hearings and depositions by agreeing to a sweeter deal.

Prosecutors can play the card similarly to encourage acceptance of their plea offer, if they have a strong victim and the parents' support. They often make veiled suggestions to the defense about the gamble associated with an accused sexual abuser of children appearing before a jury. The nature of the crime often attracts a harsher judgment from the average citizen.

But in this case, two years of plea discussions had gone nowhere, so Remland pushed forward on the deposition. In a final effort to shield the child, Hutchins made sure that Remland understood that by questioning Zoe—putting her through that trauma—there was no going back. Any plea offers were revoked; the case was going to trial. When Remland entered the depo room that day, he pushed all his chips to the center of the table.

* * *

Chuck couldn't believe how quickly he had become attached to Zoe. He and other therapy dog handlers were warned not to ask questions, not to get involved beyond their job, and to *definitely not* get attached to the people on the receiving end of animal therapy. But it was impossible in this case. Zoe reminded him of Little Orphan Annie with her light freckles and pug nose. Small for her age, she was such a contrast to the courtroom drama where the fate of people's lives was being decided. In the linoleum-paved courthouse hallways, she danced and twirled and fell all over Rikki. Like little girls are supposed to do.

He ached to think of the fate that awaited her if the case went to trial. Rikki had been used to comfort a thirteen-year-old boy a few weeks earlier, and the child was so traumatized having to face his sexual abuser that he convulsed and vomited outside the courtroom.

But from what Chuck had seen, Zoe was stronger. When they walked from the victim advocate's office to the deposition room, she had her hand on Rikki's leash, in front of Chuck's, as if they belonged together. It was as if Zoe knew Rikki was going to protect her—nothing bad was going to happen, as long as Rikki was there.

Chuck's stomach churned as he sat on the floor next to Rikki. He saw Zoe clutch the dog's head and pet her ears as if warding off thoughts of what was to come. He was impressed by how she could have such a fierce need to pet Rikki yet know not to squeeze too hard or hurt her— as the human half of an animal therapy team, Chuck's first priority was to protect his dog. It was going to be difficult for Chuck to hear the facts of the case, and he was angry about the injustice, so he tried to focus on the interaction between Zoe and Rikki rather than on what the girl or attorneys were saying.

One of Remland's initial strategies was to see if the victim had been tainted. He started, "Now, before you came here today—your mommy brought you here today, right?"

Zoe nodded her head.

"Your mom is sitting over there. See her?"

"Yes."

"She brought you here, right?"

Zoe nodded again.

"Did your mommy talk to you about this, about what was going to happen? Did she tell you anything or say what you should say or anything?"

"Yeah," she whispered.

"I'm sorry, what?"

"Yeah."

"What did your mommy tell you?"

"It was going to happen."

"Okay. And what did she say would happen? Just this?"

Zoe nodded in agreement.

"Did your mommy tell you what to say or not?"

"No."

"Before I talked to you today, when was the last time you talked about this? Do you know how long ago it was, maybe?"

Zoe shook her head.

"Was it a long time ago or last week or something?"

"A long time ago."

"A long time ago?" he repeated.

She nodded again.

When Remland wanted to know things like what happened between Mr. Frank's private parts and hers, Zoe's head disappeared under the table as she hugged Rikki. She buried her fingers and face into the dog's fur, then reappeared and replied.

Periodically during the ninety minutes of being asked the same questions different ways, Zoe reached her hand under the table for Chuck to fill it with a carrot. The dog's eyes tightly focused on the exchange, and her mouth delicately received the carrot from Zoe's palm when offered. Rikki's quiet munching added to the rhythm of the court reporter's keyboard.

By late afternoon, Remland seemed satisfied, and the men pushed their chairs away from the table. Zoe's full attention was now on Rikki, so Chuck braced himself on a chair to break free from his cage. Remaining on bent knee at Zoe's level, he touched her arm gently, met her soft blue eyes, and told her he was proud of her—she did so well. Her response came in the way of a shy smile, before she dropped her cheek to Rikki's head, dark hair draping across the fur, and wrapped her arms around for another hug.

It was after six p.m. when Chuck and Rikki exited the courthouse and he felt like he could finally breathe. Working as part of a therapy team with dying patients and those suffering from medical trauma—even his own pivotal lawsuit against Walmart in his business days—could not have prepared him mentally for what he had just endured.

How does somebody do that to a child? he wondered. He had felt so helpless in the deposition, ears ringing, head pounding. All he could think was *Oh, my God, this stuff really happened to this girl.* It wasn't until he heard her voice describing what the man did to her that he could fathom, *It actually happened. It happened to Zoe.*

It was a sense Chuck remembered feeling as a teenager when he witnessed a car wreck. He and a friend were following another vehicle into an intersection, when it stopped. Impatient, Chuck looked closer to see what the holdup was, and the scene unfolded in slow motion. A truck hauling gravel slid into the other car and turned over, its contents now a landslide, gradually erasing the car from view. Chuck's mind was frozen. *What? What am*

I seeing here? Then he realized that whoever was in that car was being buried alive.

In the deposition, it was like watching that wreck all over again. His mind froze even as his emotions flooded him. *What am I hearing? Am I really hearing this?*

Chuck dropped to one knee, wrapped his arms around Rikki, and gave in to the tears. His eyes were now open to a world that he had known existed but had never intimately experienced. It was the fallout of child sexual abuse—and here he was right in the middle of it.

It both frightened and invited Chuck, like a moth attracted to a flame. Just like when the car was crushed and he could not turn away. It was now part of his world. He had to do this—he had this dog with this incredible gift, an angel on a leash. It made too much sense; it worked so well. They had to do more of it.

CHAPTER 5

PRESCRIPTION FOR HEALING

While the prosecutor and defense attorneys were using Zoe's deposition to build their respective cases the next day, Chuck was building a case of his own. He pondered the different facilities the therapy program was serving and noted that while the teams were making a number of visits, the professionals serving those environments had not grasped their potential. Animal therapy was viewed more as a palliative treatment than as a means to promote healing.

Chuck called a friend who was in charge of continuing education at a major medical center and arranged to speak to the rehab therapists at an upcoming lunch-and-learn gathering. Three weeks later, he and Rikki were standing in front of fifteen professionals trying to convince them that dogs could play a key role in their patients' progress. As he quoted the studies and asked his listeners to recall their own experiences with animals, Chuck could tell they were making a connection—at least at the thirty-thousand-foot level. In the Q&A part of the twenty-five-minute program, though, he sensed that his audience was struggling with the practical application of animal therapy. One woman raised her hand and expressed what Chuck suspected many were thinking: "All this sounds good, but I still don't see how a dog can help my stroke patient in room 483."

Chuck looked down at Rikki and then back at the woman. "Well," he said, "why don't you let me and Rikki visit your patient after lunch?"

As he walked down the hall of the hospital rehabilitation center with the skeptical therapist, Chuck wondered how he got himself into these situations. What was he thinking? He had just put his credibility on the line, and what was about to happen in the next few minutes could make or break the relationship between the animal therapy program and its largest supporter.

The physical therapist told Chuck that her patient's left side had been affected by a stroke, but doctors thought the man could recover use if he would give therapy a chance. Unfortunately, though, he was uncooperative in physical therapy sessions. He told medical personnel it wouldn't work and insisted on using his right arm to pick up the slack for what he called his "dead arm."

When they entered the patient's room, Chuck noticed that the man's left side was facing the door. As the therapist was making introductions, Chuck was getting Rikki into position—next to the patient's left arm.

The balding man, probably in his late seventies, peered over his bedside at Rikki and smiled. Chuck dug into his pocket for a carrot and held it out in front of the dog's nose, inching her closer to the patient's arm. The man was leaning to the left, but his arm had not budged. He looked at Chuck and motioned with his right arm. "Go ahead and bring her over here to my good side, will ya?"

Chuck crouched down on one knee next to Rikki and said, "I think she's pretty happy over here. Aren't you, girl?" The dog looked briefly at Chuck, then back at the man before nuzzling the patient's left hand. Chuck saw his fingers move slightly, but his arm stayed motionless. The therapist was standing a few feet away, arms crossed, and Chuck could feel her doubt. "Let's see you give her the treat," he said, and tucked the carrot under the patient's hand. Rikki's nose moved in, and she retrieved it. The man laughed heartily, and Chuck saw his arm inch closer to the edge of the bed. Two carrots and less than ten minutes later, the man's "dead arm" was resting on the top of Rikki's head and stroking her velvety ears. Chuck grinned and looked over at the therapist, but she was so focused on the interaction that she didn't meet his eyes. Her smile told him everything he needed to know; Rikki had made another convert.

"I think I have someone else who needs to meet Rikki," the therapist told Chuck, and they offered their good-byes to the man. A few doors down, Chuck used another tactic to convince a stroke patient to take Rikki for a walk down the hallway. It was the first time the man had stood up and walked on his own since the stroke, despite weeks of rehabilitation efforts.

The following day, Chuck's e-mail in-box confirmed that his and Rikki's little experiment had paid off. The director of the rehab center wrote to say her team wanted to know when the wonder therapy dog was coming back.

News traveled to nearby facilities, and weeks later, therapy dog program coordinator Stephanie Perkins received a call from the state's largest psychiatric hospital, located in a rural community northwest of Tallahassee. A woman asked, "What can you tell us about using animal therapy teams with mental patients?"

Chuck and Stephanie traveled to meet with Florida State Hospital (FSH) administrators to introduce the concept. The planned forty-five-minute meeting ended up lasting more than four hours. As they left, Chuck told Stephanie, "They *get* it."

Within weeks, he and other human team members, Allie and Melanie Howe and Judy Sutton, started bringing their dogs for semiregular visits to the psycho-geriatric unit, where rehabilitation therapists worked with residents.

A 223-building facility on 620 acres in Chattahoochee, Florida, the FSH resembles a small city, complete with its own fire department and food services unit. It houses over two thousand people annually in two sections. The forensics section is reserved for those whom the courts determine to be "not guilty by reason of insanity" or "incompetent to proceed." The civil service section houses those who are released from forensics, those who have been committed under Florida's Baker Act (which allows for involuntary commitment), as well as people who are dually diagnosed with a mental illness and mental retardation. The FSH is the only facility in the state that serves both forensics and civil service cases. It's also unique in that it focuses on involving residents in their rehabilitation.

About six months into the program, Chuck and Rikki were scheduled to join two other teams of dogs and their people in an FSH parking lot. Rikki was snoozing on the backseat of the SUV for most of the forty-five-minute drive, but as they got closer, Chuck alerted her by saying that Rikki's "boyfriend," Grendel, would be there. He was one of the rare dogs that the golden tolerated.

At the sound of the 180-pound European Great Dane's name, Rikki's head popped up. She stretched her paws out catlike and sat up to look out the window. Rikki was part of a threesome Chuck nicknamed "The Three Stooges." It also included Grendel, who was named after the monster in a horror flick, and a retired American Kennel Club champion show dog, Caja, who has her own trophy room.

Each dog had its unique strengths. Because of his size—like that of a small pony—Grendel turned heads. He was mostly a conversation starter and helped patients by providing a source of distraction and amusement. People were usually content just watching him and asking questions. As a champion agility dog, the much smaller Caja entertained onlookers by twirling on her hind legs, jumping, rolling over, and spinning. Rikki's best trick, Chuck liked to joke, was to get a person to reach out and touch her. Even in a group setting, she found a way to zero in on the individual with the greatest need.

Once inside the building, the teams split up. Chuck followed Rikki's lead, as he had learned to trust her instincts in this type of environment better than his own. When they entered the rehab area, Rikki walked purposefully toward a patient who was sitting in front of his therapist with a vacant stare.

The therapist turned to greet Rikki, and she acknowledged him with a swish of her tail, then sat down next to his patient. Picking up on her cue, the therapist told Chuck the patient's name was Arnold. Chuck bent down next to his dog and said, "This is Rikki and she's a therapy dog. Would you like to meet her?" Arnold didn't acknowledge them but looked toward a woman who was

standing next to the therapist. She made some hand sig-
nals, so Chuck guessed that Arnold must be deaf. After
the exchange, Arnold's answer to the request came in
the form of a shooing motion toward Chuck and Rikki.
Chuck smiled and stood up. "That's all right," he said, and
shrugged. He thanked the therapist and the interpreter
before steering Rikki in another direction.

The next four residents were much more interested,
and Rikki charmed them for a few minutes before trying
to lead Chuck back toward Arnold. Chuck followed her
lead, thinking maybe the man had changed his mind. As
they came closer, Arnold didn't look their way and dismissed them with a wave of his hand.

Chuck led Rikki to other therapist-patient groups,
and she was attentive, but then tried to pull Chuck toward
Arnold a third time. This time, he didn't bother to wave
them away. He stared at the therapist while Chuck knelt
down and stroked Rikki's head, hoping to get Arnold's
attention. After a few minutes, Chuck whispered to Rikki,
"Little girl, I think we need to leave him alone," and stood
up. She slowly followed her owner's lead across the room.
A few minutes later, Rikki pulled in Arnold's direction
again.

Chuck resigned himself to his dog's insistence. He had
learned to trust Rikki's gift of discerning who in a room
needed to meet her, even if only she knew why. He got
the attention of the interpreter. "Forgive me, but my dog
really seems to think that your client would like to meet

her. Would you mind asking him just one more time?" Before the woman answered, they both saw that Rikki had planted herself at Arnold's feet and was looking straight up toward his face expectantly. Arnold glanced down briefly and then suddenly started thrashing his arms, as if he were experiencing a seizure. Chuck quickly knelt down next to Rikki and wrapped his finger around her collar, in case he needed to get her out of the way. But she stayed focused on Arnold, her muscles relaxed and mouth open in a sort of grin.

Chuck watched as a rapid series of expressions cycled across Arnold's face and his eyes rolled back. Seconds later, his look softened and his mouth formed a smile. He turned fully toward Rikki and reached out to her as if she were a new discovery. Chuck felt Rikki moving closer and watched as Arnold leaned over and wrapped his arms around her neck, burying his head in her fur and moaning. Rikki was relaxed and leaned into him as if returning the embrace. Chuck, the therapist, and the interpreter watched in stunned silence as Arnold wept softly and rocked back and forth, holding the dog.

Then as rapidly as it started, Arnold suddenly released Rikki and sat upright, looking straight ahead. His vacant stare returned. Chuck waited for a moment, then felt Rikki stand up, so he also stood. She quietly started walking toward the exit, and Chuck followed, giving a casual wave to the interpreter, still speechless because of the exchange. All he could think was *What just happened?*

When he started down the hallway, Chuck saw that Arnold's therapist was following them. He also had a look of amazement. He told Chuck that Arnold suffered from dissociative identity disorder. During his twelve years at the Florida State Hospital, staff had identified nine distinct personalities. However, Arnold's dominant one—which was aloof and antisocial—controlled the others and prevented them from emerging, so they would only get glimpses of them on occasion.

Then he told Chuck, "Your dog did in a few minutes what I haven't been able to do in twelve years. She connected with one of his personalities who wanted to deal with the outside world in a positive manner."

Chuck said he had experienced some unusual encounters with his therapy dog, but this one was especially unique. The therapist said he had heard of animal-assisted therapy but had never really believed it could benefit his practice. He asked if Chuck and Rikki could return soon and work exclusively with Arnold. "Absolutely," Chuck said. "I'm as anxious as you are to see where it might lead."

Chuck and Rikki arrived for the scheduled visit a few weeks later, and when they walked into the therapy room, he realized there were a few more people than usual. He recognized one woman as the chief medical director, and his stomach tensed. It appeared that he and Rikki were there to prove themselves to a skeptical audience.

Aware that dogs can pick up on their handlers' cues and mirror their feelings, Chuck tried his best to suppress his nervousness. Rikki's relaxed walk around the room as she lured people to pet her assured him she was fine.

Still, he couldn't help but wonder, *Will this work?* Since he had no idea how it happened the first time, he didn't have a clue whether Rikki would be able to connect with Arnold again. He reminded himself about the hundreds of other successful interactions they'd had together and decided to let go of his worries about the session's outcome.

Arnold sat facing his therapist and interpreter, but as with the first visit, he was uninterested. For an hour, Chuck knelt on the floor next to the dog, until his legs started going numb. Usually, when there was a lull in activity, Rikki would sprawl out on the floor—she could sleep anywhere. But this time she remained upright, within petting distance, her attention fully on Arnold.

Finally, "Earl," the name given to the personality who wanted to pet Rikki, emerged. The transition was obvious. It was like a different person taking over the same body, with entirely different expressions. His face went from a stern defiance to a softer openness, and he turned toward Rikki and reached out to stroke her fur.

Chuck marveled as new personalities emerged, six distinct ones—including one that didn't want to pet Rikki but seemed to enjoy watching Chuck pet her. He asked questions through his interpreter.

As he was encouraging the interaction between Rikki and Arnold, Chuck heard the medical director whisper to one of her colleagues, "He's never done *anything* like this before." She later said she was especially impressed that Arnold had acknowledged a visitor—Chuck—and, even more so, that he had asked him questions.

Seeing how Chuck caught Rikki's attention with carrots, Arnold reached for one. He held it out to Rikki and smiled at the gentle retrieving and quiet munching that followed. Chuck pulled another carrot from his pocket and asked Rikki to "shake." She quickly offered her right paw and leaned forward to claim her reward. Out of the corner of his eye, Chuck saw Arnold's face contort when another personality tried to emerge, but the personality petting Rikki shooed it away, as if it were a mosquito. Chuck noted that Rikki knew when to move in and engage with Arnold and when to give him distance.

Rikki extended her head and parted her lips in a smile, as Arnold stroked her ears and made a soft cooing sound. The therapist asked Arnold basic questions, trying to engage him in gentle conversation. He answered through his interpreter, keeping his hands on Rikki when he wasn't signing.

After about ninety minutes, the therapist said it was time to go and asked if they could walk Chuck and Rikki to the car. As they exchanged thanks, including Arnold through his interpreter, Chuck felt his throat clench with emotion at what seemed like a miracle. He said he appreciated their giving Rikki and him a chance to help.

Barely out of sight of the hospital, Chuck looked into his rearview mirror and saw that Rikki had fallen into a deep slumber across the backseat. Sharing so much of herself had tired her out.

On their regular visit the following month, as the teams entered the specialty care unit, Chuck saw Arnold, who no longer had the vacant expression. Instead, he was holding a notepad, communicating with his therapist through written word in addition to using the interpreter. Chuck thought for sure Arnold would recognize them, but he didn't even look their way. Looking down at Rikki, Chuck waited for her to start pulling in Arnold's direction. But it was the same; neither seemed particularly interested in the other.

Chuck was both disappointed and confused, until he pondered it further: Arnold didn't need Rikki anymore, and she knew it. He needed a way to get around his detached dominant personality, which kept him in solitary confinement in his own body. Rikki's gift had helped unlock the cell door. And now his therapists could treat him using more traditional methods.

CHAPTER 6

COURTHOUSE COMFORT

Assistant State Attorney John Hutchins and Victim Advocate Susan Parmalee remained in contact with Zoe's parents as the case progressed over three years. By fall 2009, four different trial dates had been set, all of them delayed.

Susan called Danielle to tell her the court had set a new trial date in November. Danielle said fine, as long as it was not on Zoe's birthday, which was on a Monday that year. The court always held jury selection on Mondays, Susan told her, so that would not be an issue. She asked that Danielle keep her schedule open for a trial later the same week.

The afternoon of Zoe's birthday, Danielle had just picked up the children from school when Susan called. "John and I need to meet with you immediately," she said in a tone that was all business. Danielle's first thought was *Frank Dieter doesn't want to face this and has killed himself.* Susan said she could not go into detail on the phone, so Danielle arranged for them to meet at her mother-in-law's house. That way she'd have someone to watch Zoe and her little brother while they talked.

Danielle wondered what they could possibly need to tell her that was so urgent. She kept imagining worst-case scenarios, like that Frank had somehow managed to get the charges dropped. John and Susan took a seat in the living room, and they made some small talk, mostly about Danielle's pregnancy. She was four and a half months along and was clearly showing.

After a brief pause, Danielle looked over at John, who she knew would deliver the news. He was a big man with broad shoulders, and Danielle remembered how when they first met she had been concerned that his size might scare her daughter. But every time John talked to Zoe, he bent down on one knee, closer to her level, and spoke to her in gentle tones. He also had big, kind eyes, so that's what Danielle focused on.

"I'm really sorry," John said. Danielle felt as if her heart had stopped when he paused. "But we are going to have to delay the trial again."

Danielle felt like screaming. Inside, she wanted to yell and fly into a rage. Instead, she heard herself calmly reply, "Okay."

John met her eyes and studied her demeanor. "That's it?" he said. "You don't seem very upset."

Danielle sighed deeply. "What can I do?"

John said he could understand her frustration. "Just have faith in us. We will get there; we will make sure Frank Dieter is held accountable." John didn't want to make any promises, because he had no control over the outcome. But they had plenty of evidence, and the cause for the delay would add to the prosecution's case. The crime lab had found Frank's DNA on Zoe's pajamas and therefore initially had not tested the other articles collected from the scene—sheets and panties. But the defense attorney had hired a DNA expert witness and so the court had requested that all articles be tested.

Susan said she would keep Danielle posted on the new trial date, which would likely not be until after the first of the year. And she did. In fact, Susan would contact her two more times about trial dates that were set, then postponed—one by the prosecution and the other by the defense—before both sides agreed the first week in April would work.

All efforts turned toward preparing Zoe to take the witness stand. The court was asking a lot of the eight-year-old: she would have to answer questions in front of a judge and jury, recall events of the crime—even if she didn't understand what they meant—and do all of this in the presence of the man she knew as "Mr. Frank," once her parents' best friend.

Susan arranged for Danielle to bring Zoe to the courthouse a few times before the trial so that she could have positive interactions there, making the trial less traumatic. During one visit, Susan gave Zoe a coloring book featuring a typical courtroom so she could see where the judge would sit and where she as the witness would sit. They brought her into the same courtroom where the trial was going to take place and let her practice talking into the microphone. John even asked her a few questions, including having her spell her name, so she could see how the microphone worked.

The next "practice session" was scheduled for the day before the trial. John was going to be asking Zoe specifics about the incident, so he needed her to try to remember as many details as possible. He and Susan decided it might help for Zoe to watch her videotaped forensics interview, which took place forty-eight hours after the rape. Knowing that it might be difficult for Zoe, Susan called to see if Chuck and Rikki would be available.

Earlier that spring, Chuck had suspended most of his animal therapy visits because of a failed ankle surgery. He was scheduled for an ankle-replacement surgery in May and, in the meantime, was using a cane to get around. Still, when Susan called, he said, "It's not a matter of whether I'll be able to make it, but how."

The afternoon of the meeting, Chuck's wife, Patty, dropped him and Rikki off at the front door of the courthouse, and he hobbled through the doors. A deputy looked up at Chuck, then down at Rikki, smiled, and waved them in—not even bothering to check his pack.

Susan, Zoe, and her younger brother, Eli, came into the courthouse rotunda to escort Rikki and Chuck upstairs. As the kids took turns feeding the dog carrots, Susan told Chuck that Danielle, now nearly nine months pregnant, was waiting for them in the victim advocate office.

When they arrived upstairs, Chuck and Rikki kept the two kids entertained briefly, until Danielle could steer Eli into the toy area. Susan turned to Zoe and asked if she wanted to see a video in which she was the star.

She looked up at Chuck. "Can Rikki come?"

He smiled. "Of course."

Walking into her office, Susan said, "Zoe, why don't you have a seat in my chair." Once she was settled into the office chair, Chuck handed her a small bag of carrots, in case she wanted to treat Rikki. He then lowered himself carefully to the floor on the other side of the dog, keeping his ankle outstretched and cane nearby.

Zoe folded her leg under herself to better see the computer monitor, swiveled the chair slightly, and rested a hand on Rikki. She told Susan she was ready.

* * *

It was two days after the incident, and Danielle had brought five-year-old Zoe to the child protection team office for a forensics interview. Program Supervisor Kimberly Ellis led Zoe into a room stocked with colorful cans of Play-Doh, crayons, and coloring books.

"I'm on the child protection team," Kim told her, "and I talk to boys and girls who are at least four all the way up to big kids, age seventeen, about lots of secret stuff. And so we're going to do a little bit of talking today. Okay?"

She asked Zoe's name and age, then what day it was— the last of which Zoe did not know.

"While we're talking today, I might ask you some questions like I've already started doing. And if you don't know the answer, it's okay; you just tell me you don't know, like you just said, right? You said you didn't know the date, and believe me, that's fine. If you don't know something, you just tell me you don't know, okay?"

Kim pulled out some crayons, and Zoe demonstrated that she knew her colors. She counted them, too, up to nine. Zoe shared that at preschool she had learned a song in which they counted backward, and then began singing:

Somewhere in outer space
God has prepared a place
For those who trust him and obey
Jesus will come again
Although we don't know when
The countdown's getting closer every day

Ten and nine, eight and seven, six and five and four
Count upon the Savior while you may
Three and two comin' through the clouds in bright
array
The countdown's getting lower every day

Kim complimented her on the song, then offered her some Play-Doh to work with while they visited. "Okay. Now, Zoe, tell me a little about you. I've never seen you before. You told me that you go to day care, and you told me your teacher's name is Ms. . . ."

"Dottie," Zoe answered. She told Kim that her "bubbie" lived at home with her and clarified that he wasn't a grown-up; he was a child.

"Tell me some things you do at day care," Kim said.

"I play with babies and dolphins."

"Babies and dolphins, okay. What else do you guys do there?"

"We do lots of work."

"Lots of work, like what kind of work?"

"Writing."

Kim asked what she liked about day care and what she didn't like about it, then said, "Zoe, do you know why you came to see me today? Do you know what it's about?"

The child nodded.

"What's it about?"

"Mr. Frank."

"Mr. Frank? Tell me about Mr. Frank."

"A few days ago I went to his house, and he—I don't remember."

"You don't remember?"

"I can't remember what I did."

"Okay, well, let's see. Is Mr. Frank a kid or a grown-up?"

"He is a grown-up."

"He is a grown-up, okay. Do you know who lives at Mr. Frank's house?"

"Ms. Heather."

"Ms. Heather, okay. Are there any kids at Mr. Frank's house?"

"He doesn't have kids."

"He doesn't have kids, okay."

Kim changed the subject for a moment, then came back to the topic.

"So tell me some more about Mr. Frank. Tell me something that Mr. Frank does that you like."

"He gives me treats."

"He gives you treats, okay."

"My mommy and daddy tells him that we can't have treats."

Zoe said Mr. Frank watched kid movies with them and they recently watched *The Polar Express*. She said she sometimes went to his house, and Kim asked if he ever came to hers.

"Uh-huh, but he is not anymore."

"He is not anymore? How come?"

"Because he did something to me."

"He did something to you?"

"When I was sleeping he did, my blanket."

"What did he do to you?"

"He stuck his pee-pee into my bottom."

"He stuck his pee-pee into your bottom? Sometimes boys and girls tell me about that kind of stuff, Zoe. Tell me some more about that so that I understand what you're talking about. Where were you when that happened?"

"In my bed."

"In your bed? So is that at your house?"

She nodded her head and said her mommy and daddy were out getting groceries.

"What were you wearing when that happened?" Kim asked.

"My pj's."

"Your pj's? Now, Zoe, I have never seen your pj's, so tell me some more about them. What do they look like?"

"They're old ones and they're new ones. One's a precious one, and one—the one that I wear the night before—it was . . . it was a snake on a tree. That's when he did that."

Zoe said Mr. Frank also did this at his house when her daddy wasn't looking and sometimes used his finger in her "pee-pee."

"And what does he do when he puts his finger in your pee-pee?"

"He does it back and forth."

Kim repeated her description, and Zoe's nod confirmed it. "Okay. Does he touch your pee-pee with anything else?"

"No. Just his finger and his pee-pee."

When asked for a description of his privates, Zoe said it looked like a boy pee-pee. And that he put his "slobber" from his mouth on it.

"What does he say to you?" Kim asked.

"Well, he said, 'Don't tell anyone.'"

Kim needed to clarify what had occurred in the most recent instance two days before, so she asked, "What did he touch your pee-pee with that last time?"

"His pee-pee. He didn't touch my pee-pee when I was in bed. He touched my bottom when I was in bed."

"Okay. Just your bottom when you were in bed, okay. And that was with his finger—is that right?"

"No. His pee-pee."

"His pee-pee, okay. And what did he do with his pee-pee that time?"

"He just hit it up and down in there."

Kim reached for some anatomical drawings of a little girl and a "grown-up boy." She had Zoe point to the parts of the body that correspond with "pee-pee"—his and hers—and "bottom," and the parts he had touched.

"Where did he touch you with his finger?"

"Inside."

"Okay. Can you mark inside where it was?"

Zoe made a mark.

"What part of his body did he touch your pee-pee with? Can you circle it for me?"

Zoe pointed.

"Okay. What did he touch your bottom with?" Zoe pointed again. "That same part? Okay."

Kim clarified that the reference was to the last time it happened at her house, and Zoe volunteered, "The police took my sheet away. I got a Tinker Bell sheet." Zoe said she tried to keep him off the sheets, and Kim asked, "When Mr. Frank left, were your sheets dry or wet or something else?"

"It was wet."

"Do you know how it got wet?"

"His pee-pee made it wet."

Kim told Zoe she could play with the Play-Doh while she went out of the room to check on something. When she came back, she said, "Did you think of anything else that I might need to know about? Anything else maybe that Mr. Frank said to you?"

"He didn't say nothing, but I know why he did that."

"You do? Why do you think he did that?"

"Because he liked me."

Next, Kim introduced a game to Zoe that involved a crayon being inside of a bucket and outside to demonstrate that she knew the difference, and then told her, "You know what, Ms. Zoe? I think that I am done asking you questions. Unless there's anything else you think

I should know about. Is there anything else that Mr. Frank does that you don't like?"

Zoe nodded her head up and down. "I don't like him sticking his pee-pee into my bottom."

* * *

Susan stepped forward, reached around the side of Zoe, and closed the video screen. She crouched down next to Rikki and looked right at the girl. "Do you think you can talk about the things from the video in front of other people?"

Zoe dropped her head to one side as if pondering the question further, then answered, "I can if Rikki's there."

CHAPTER 7

READING HOOD

While five-year-old Rikki was Chuck's canine partner working as a courthouse therapy dog and visiting hospitals and rehab centers, her big brother, Roscoe, was partnered with Patty in the schools.

Patty and Roscoe had become a certified animal therapy team through the Delta Society (an organization now known as Pet Partners) and then completed the Reading Education Assistance Dogs (READ) training. She read the manual, watched a DVD series, and attended a workshop at the Intermountain Therapy Animals headquarters in Utah for certification. After shadowing other READ teams locally as part of the practical application, she and Roscoe became regular volunteers at Cornerstone Learning

Community, a private school for pre-K through eighth-grade students. The happy Lab was fine in the school's ultrastimulating environment, a reading area between classrooms with a constant flow of kids, but Patty noticed he became fidgety in other learning centers where they were isolated in smaller, quiet rooms. Just like his human counterparts, he needed activity to keep him engaged.

After Chuck was sidelined with the ankle injury, he suggested Patty try Rikki in schools the following academic year. She wasn't sure at first, because Rikki didn't do well around crowds of children, but Chuck pointed out that what mattered was the one-on-one interactions. Patty decided to introduce Rikki to an after-school program and test her out. She was impressed that Rikki maintained the same calm demeanor around the children at the busy center that she had in the much quieter courts. It was enough to convince Patty to have Rikki evaluated for READ as well.

Once Chuck became mobile again, the couple started coordinating their weekly schedules. Rikki was reading with kids on Wednesdays and visiting patients in a number of medical environments with Chuck on Thursdays. Roscoe was officially retired.

* * *

At nine a.m. on a Wednesday, early in the school year, Patty navigated her red Prius hybrid with the "Save a friend's life—adopt a dog" bumper sticker into the Cornerstone parking lot. In the backseat, Rikki started panting in anticipation. She snoozed most of the forty minutes it took for Patty to drive from one end of the county to the other, but in the last five minutes of the trip, Rikki seemed to recognize the driving pattern and sat up to study the passing landscape. Perhaps it was the stop-and-go rhythms of traffic lights—Patty wasn't sure—but Rikki definitely knew when they were getting close to the school.

Rikki's routine the previous day had put her on alert: bath, ear cleaning, and long strokes across her thick orange coat with a Furminator to reduce shedding. There was the curtailed freedom, too. She was not allowed to linger on the two acres of fenced yard; she had to do her business and come right back into the house.

Patty's uniform for the day included a tan-colored "Wild About R.E.A.D." T-shirt, off-white loose-fitting slacks, and J-41 recycled-leather shoes. A blue wallet-type ID badge with pictures of her and Rikki dangled from a cord on her neck. In the photo, you could see a hint of Patty's half-Hawaiian heritage—the tawny skin tone, big moon-shaped brown eyes, and short nose.

Not that anyone would notice her. When Patty was with Rikki, she seemed to disappear.

That's something she and Chuck laughed about when sharing stories after working with their dogs in the class-rooms, courts, and hospitals. She and Rikki visited the same places and saw the same people, week after week. Yet Patty suspected that very few of them—adults or kids—would be able to recall her name. What they remembered was that she was "Rikki's mom."

Patty opened the back door of the car and snapped a red leash peppered with paw prints to Rikki's collar. The dog stepped purposefully onto the pavement like a celebrity carefully calculating her steps. The five tags on her collar collided in a quiet jingle. There was the red heart engraved with her name and the Mitchells' phone number, a blue polygon indicating that she had received the rabies vaccine, a round red medal identifying her as a READ dog, a green, white, and black plastic disk certifying that she was an official Delta Society Pet Partner, and another red heart with her 24PetWatch microchip number and a toll-free number to call if she was ever lost. A red bandana tied loosely around her neck was emblazoned with the READ logo.

Rikki surveyed the surroundings and heard the blend of giggles and shouts from the nearby playground. Her mouth first closed in concentration, then loosened again in a smile. Her just-brushed tail began its gentle sweeping motion.

Patty opened the gate on the green chain-link fence for Rikki to enter on their way to check in at the office. Two girls abandoned the swing set and came to pet the long-haired golden, who stood calmly for the affection.

Patty paused momentarily, greeted one of the teachers, then turned, with Rikki matching her step.

Cornerstone Learning Community, with only 170 students, resides in three buildings connected by a railed wooden boardwalk and heavily shaded playgrounds. The main office faces the road, blocking the rest of the campus from view. Its screened back porch is a remnant from its previous use as a single-family home.

As soon as Patty was inside the door, the office staff recognized her, but their attention was quickly diverted to Rikki. Their voices rose a few notes, and Rikki, tuned into the familiar singsong tone, responded with a sway of her tail.

Patty and Rikki were working with the younger students at the school, so the two left the office and followed the boardwalk to the east house, a southern-architecture cottage with a wraparound screened porch that makes it look more like a beach hideaway than a school.

Rikki and Patty's home for the next two hours would be the library, a wide hallway between the boys' and girls' restrooms. Everything about the space said *kids welcome here.* Surfaces spilled over with collections of books. In an oblong white wicker basket colorfully labeled "Books On Hold," the titles awaiting their next reader included a book from the DK Readers Star Wars: The Clone Wars series, *Ricky Ricotta's Mighty Robot,* and *Dogs Rule!*

Soft- and hardbacks sat upright and sideways on shelves—some anchored by red, blue, pink, and green plastic bins containing a subset of the collection. A desk on one side of the room had a computer monitor, a keyboard, and a phone, but all were nearly buried by colorfully painted buckets containing school office essentials (scissors, clothespins), pump bottles of hand sanitizer, more books, and yellow stickies. A Paddington Bear lamp peeked out from behind the buckets, while overhead a series of floating shelves draped with white mini Christmas lights served as seating for stuffed versions of a range of story-time favorites, from Piglet and the Cat in the Hat to Peter Rabbit.

Patty unfolded a three-by-four-foot pad to map out her reading space, while Rikki stood patiently watching and waiting. The center of the floor had been covered with a portable protective surface in a colorful speckled pattern that resembled a kid's painting.

They were scheduled to work with first graders, and soon a brown-haired boy named Luke came strolling into the room, carrying a flexible plastic tote with several books, mostly about animals.

He walked over and placed a hand on Rikki's back in greeting before settling in next to "Miss Patty." Rikki sat for a moment, then lowered herself down and used her front paws as a pillow.

Luke turned to look at Rikki, as if acknowledging his audience, then pulled out a book about a cat and began.

"My cat loo-ks . . ."

Patty pointed to the word. "There's the 'i,' so we make the 'i' sound."

He added, "And the 'l.'"

She encouraged him. "So, my cat . . ."

Luke caught on. "*Likes* to play with me."

Patty pointed to the picture. "What is she playing with?"

"A yo-yo."

"Uh-huh, and this is s-t-r-i-n-g-s, strings."

"Strings."

She pointed to the photo. "Look at her beautiful eyes."

He continued, "My cat likes to hide . . . in the grass."

Again, Patty pointed. "Is that what she's doing?"

He protested, "But my dad covers the pictures!"

"Do you want me to, also?"

"Uh-huh."

Patty complied for the balance of the fifteen-minute session. As Luke said good-bye, she reminded him that he had asked for another of Rikki's personal business cards. She dug it out of her book bag. One side of the card was a photo of Rikki draped in a blue patterned bandana, with her name in large letters: "Rikki Mitchell." The other side gave details about the animal-assisted therapy program, Rikki's Delta Society therapy dog team number, plus a list of some of the institutions she visited for therapy services—the Second Judicial Circuit of Florida; Tallahassee Memorial Hospital, Rehabilitation Center, and Behavioral Health Center; Florida State Hospital; and the READ program at Leon County Schools. The bottom read, "Contact my partner, Chuck Mitchell, Delta Certified Therapy Team Evaluator," followed by his e-mail and cell phone number.

Luke studied the business card and asked if Miss Patty had one with Rikki wearing a red bandana like what she's wearing today, but she told him she only had the one with the blue. His voice rose with the next question: "Can I give her a carrot?" Patty handed him one. Rikki gently retrieved it from his palm, and the boy reached out his hand to Patty again. "How much more?"

It would be a three-carrot visit.

Melanie's turn was next, and Luke was in charge of fetching her—"After you wash your hands," Patty told him.

"Good morning, Melanie," Patty said, in her best adult-addressing-a-kid tone. Melanie was a picture of pastels, with her soft strawberry hair, teal smock blouse, cord necklace with a round green pendant, and color-coordinated plastic ring on her left pointer finger. Like Luke, she was carrying a plastic tote with books.

"You've got a whole bunch of things in your bag today," Patty said, and Melanie acknowledged her with a drop of her forehead and a shy smile.

Melanie looked toward Rikki, who had sunk into a full supine position, then knelt down and reached for her reading glasses. From the pastel-blue case, she pulled out rose-colored frames and began delicately wiping the lenses with a cloth.

Patty asked what she'd like to read, and Melanie's response was whisper soft. Patty caught a barely audible "cat" and assured her that Rikki liked cat stories.

Melanie began, sounding out each word. As she concentrated, she pushed her tongue beyond her jagged front tooth and gripped it between her lips. Between pages, she tugged on her feet, which were bound in leather sandals with a large metallic peace sign.

When Melanie reached the middle of the book, some third graders who had taken a detour from the girls' bathroom to pet Rikki interrupted her. But Patty told them they would have to visit when the session was over.

Next, Melanie selected a book from the Danny series, which features photographs of a yellow Labrador retriever named Danny instead of illustrations. Before she opened it, Melanie leaned over to scratch Rikki's head.

She began, "Playing with Abby. Danny and Abby play . . ." Melanie looked up in recognition. "Abby's in my class."

"Do I know Abby?" Patty asked. "Maybe you can show me who she is. Oh." Patty pointed to an inside page and said in an impressive tone, "This has more than seventy-four words."

Melanie began again. "Danny and Abby are resting on the deck."

Patty told her that Rikki and her brother, Roscoe, rest on the deck at their home, then looked at Rikki. "Yeah, she likes the Danny books."

Melanie followed her glance and observed, "She's sleeping."

"No, she's not," Patty corrected. "She's listening, because she loves the sound of your voice."

After Melanie finished reading the Danny and Abby book, Patty told her, "You did a great job today. Are you feeling pretty comfortable reading to Rikki?"

Melanie nodded.

"It looks like it. Would you like to give her some carrots? How about three carrots—I think she's due." Patty reminded the girl to offer the carrot with a flat hand. Melanie, a little eager, tried to give Rikki more while she was still munching, but Patty intervened. "We'll wait 'til she's done eating."

Some kids walked by and tried to linger, but Patty corrected them. "I think they're missing you in the classroom!"

* * *

Launched by Intermountain Therapy Animals (ITA) in Salt Lake City, Utah, in 1999, the READ program was the first comprehensive literacy-support program built around the idea of having children read to dogs. What prompted the founders—a registered nurse and a librarian—was the realization that learning to read seemed like less of an intellectual process than one about overcoming fears. Especially the fear of public failure, as children must demonstrate their reading ability by reading in front of their classmates. Animals were found to be ideal reading companions, because they help children to relax. The founders discovered studies going back as far as the 1970s that showed that children's blood pressure and heart rate decrease when they read to a dog. The presence of the animal draws their attention away from their own anxieties and makes them feel safe. And because dogs appear to listen attentively—they do not judge, laugh, or criticize— the children can go at their own pace, without interruption. The animals are also much less intimidating than the child's peers.

As with Chuck's animal-assisted therapy work, READ handlers used a dog's strengths to promote interaction with the child. One handler taught her dog to "point" to a page by placing her paw on it when she gave verbal cues. She would then tell the child the dog wanted to hear that part of the story again. Another had her dog cock his head as if he didn't understand—so the child would be asked to repronounce a word.

Each school year brought a new crop of success stories.

One of Patty's favorite recollections was Grace Jackson, who met with Patty and Roscoe every Wednesday during second grade at Cornerstone. The girl grew to love reading so much that she started writing her own stories and poems, one of which was published a year later.

Grace autographed Patty's copy of *Unspoiled: Writers Speak for Florida's Coast,* which includes her poem. Above her signature, Grace wrote, "You have helped me progress in my reading very much. Your hard work really paid off. You made reading fun for me." Next to the message, the girl drew a picture of a dog. She signed it, "Love, Grace (the one who never wears matching socks)."

Practicing reading is the primary focus of READ, but if the setting allows, Patty will introduce anything related to learning, such as looking at a map of the world or doing the child's homework.

Some settings, like public schools, are more institutional and discourage hugging or sitting too close to children. With the rest, Patty just goes with the flow. If a kid reaches up to hug, she hugs back. That's how the program goes beyond teaching reading and really changes hearts, Chuck likes to say.

Although the human team members are warned not to get too involved with the children, some handlers admit to taking on assignments not related to their work. When a boy showed up at his after-school program in beat-up socks and no shoes, one READ volunteer learned that his shoes had become too small. No one at his house seemed to notice that he wasn't wearing shoes when he left for school. The READ volunteer used her hand to measure his foot, and after the session she raced to the shoe store to get him some new sneakers.

Other needs are less obvious, so Patty and her fellow READ pet handlers talk with teachers to determine strategies to help particular students. And in a typical school year, those needs are ever changing.

When Patty and Rikki arrived at a school one day, Patty was told not to expect much from one of her students, because he was emotionally shut down; his father had committed suicide two days before. Patty kept the appointment with the boy, allowing extra time for him to just be with Rikki and talk, if he felt like it. To Patty's surprise, he talked about his feelings to the dog. Later, the teachers told Patty that he opened up to them afterward as well. Once his emotions stabilized, he was able to focus on school again.

Stories like that of the grief-stricken boy have taught the READ coordinators to be open to whatever benefits the dog teams can offer. One after-school program coordinator told Patty the warmth and comfort of the READ instructors is a rare source of love and stability in some kids' lives.

* * *

One afternoon at three thirty, Patty and Rikki arrived at the Character Center, an academic-based after-school program. Strawberry-scented air freshener lingered in the entranceway. After checking in with co-owner Zack Richardson, Patty and Rikki followed a short hallway to the Maggie Mae READ Room. The space was named for one of Rikki's fellow READ canines. Maggie Mae's handler, Shirley Roux, and her husband, Ken, had decorated the space when the Character Center moved in.

The room was an ideal environment for children to read, with big, puffy floor pillows, a child-sized table with two chairs, bookshelves, and—best of all—a door that you could close to avoid interruptions and noise. READ teams were visiting the center four days a week, and they hoped to have the fifth day covered soon.

Before Patty and Rikki's first appointment, kids paraded by and Patty recognized each one. "I think you grew an inch since last week—you're almost as tall as I am . . . although"—she chuckled—"I'm not that tall."

In her three years visiting the Character Center, Patty had collected stories on just about every student. One involved a now third grader named Jeffrey who had become her "book reviewer"; his job was to determine if a book topic seemed appropriate for other students. She even asked him to review a story about one of NFL quarterback Michael Vick's dogs, Audie, who had survived severe abuse while training for and engaging in dogfights.

Jeffrey suffered from a speech impediment that caused him to mispronounce words, which led to embarrassment in class. He started reading to Rikki at the end of first grade, and within a year, he was reading aloud better than many adults—the words just flowing off his tongue. Jeffrey sometimes paused over words like "agility" or "competition," but he sounded them out first and then nailed them the second time. His retention was obvious, too. After reading the first paragraph of *Saving Audie: A Pit Bull Puppy Gets a Second Chance*, he asked, "Okay, but how do you even fight a dog in a dog fight?"

"You know, I wish I could answer that question for you," Patty said. "But let me tell you this. When dogs are afraid, they will bite, and so these dogs are not given water or food, and they're chained outside, and they're not treated well. So they're always scared. People will bring the two dogs together, and they will do what any dog would do if they were facing something they feared. They would start fighting."

Steering the conversation back to the book, she said, "But we're not going to focus on the fighting; we're going to focus on saving Audie."

Later Jeffrey wondered why the dogs were kept as evidence of the crime.

"'Evidence,' do you know what that means?" Patty asked.

He didn't even hesitate. "To prove something."

She told him that Audie would be cared for by rescuers and then adopted out to a loving home after the court case.

Jeffrey pondered her answer, then started scratching his arm. He said he had Eskimo.

"Eskimo?"

He scratched again and pointed to a patch of flaky skin near his wrist.

"Oh, eczema. I understand what you are saying."

CHAPTER 8

NO DOGS ALLOWED

In the far reaches of the county, the morning had gotten off to a rocky start for Chuck Mitchell. Ankle-replacement surgery was still three weeks away, and his daily routines could be difficult. He hadn't slept well the previous three nights, and his stomach was in knots anticipating Zoe's trial that day. Testifying in court could be brutal for children. Kids often have nightmares and even get physically ill prior to facing their abuser in the courtroom. Chuck was hoping it would be different for Zoe.

He swung his feet to the floor and sat on the edge of the bed. Chuck wasn't taking the pain pills his doctor had prescribed, because he didn't want to risk getting fuzzy headed; he needed to have all his wits about him.

He grabbed his cane, stood up, and winced, then hobbled across the room. At least he was spared having to navigate the steep staircase. Years before, they had installed a residential elevator for his mother-in-law in an unused closet area. Though she had only used it once or twice, times like this made him thankful for their investment.

Patty was already on her way downstairs, and Chuck could hear the dogs barking and whimpering to go outside. "Keep an eye on Rikki for me," he called from their bedroom. Patty understood what he meant. Roscoe loved to dig, and Rikki, thinking it a game, was usually on the receiving end of his dirt clods.

When Chuck got to the main floor and entered the kitchen, he started assembling Rikki's backpack: baby carrot treats in several Ziplocs so Zoe wouldn't give them all to her at once, a high-value treat of miniature dog biscuits in case Rikki got distracted, bottled water, a portable water bowl, and poop bags—even though in five years he had never had to pick up after Rikki in public.

Chuck opened the door to let the dogs back into the house, and Rikki's tail swayed in a warm greeting, until she spied the pack on the counter. Suddenly, she was in a full frenzy, prancing toward the pack and then over to Chuck, tail wagging vigorously. With the previous day's routine of bath, brushing, and teeth and ear cleaning, she knew it was a workday, and her whole body seemed to be saying, "Bring it on."

Watching Rikki's reaction helped ease the tension in Chuck's stomach. He had built a construction company from scratch, rescued another from bankruptcy, and even constructed their home with his bare hands—but he still felt woefully unprepared for what he was about to face.

Zoe had been so competent in their previous meetings—the deposition, pretrial hearings, and the previous day's trial prep. But what they were facing now was serious. They were done with the pop quizzes—this was the final exam. Zoe would have to keep it together while she was in that courtroom in order for justice to be served.

The night before, Chuck had asked his wife, "How can I keep Rikki focused on Zoe?" Patty answered in her usual mellow manner, "Just let her do her thing."

Chuck had arranged to park in a friend's law office lot, which was only a short walk from the Leon County Courthouse and would make the going a little easier. But the cane he had used the day before didn't give him the kind of control he needed, so even though it was painful, he was going to try to forgo the cane, use a leg brace, and just hope for the best.

The important thing was to keep Rikki from keying in on his pain, which would be nearly impossible with her uncanny ability to identify hurting people. She had a compassion radar that wasn't easily deterred.

After Chuck parked the SUV with the "3DOG DAD" license plate, he limped up the hill with Rikki—tail taut, all-business mode—in the lead. Chuck managed to get through the first set of heavy glass doors, and the deputy—one Chuck didn't know—saw his struggle and pushed open the second one. Okay, the day was getting better.

When they arrived at Susan Parmalee's office, Rikki instantly shifted her compassion toward Zoe, who burst around the corner with outstretched arms and yelled, "Rikki!" The dog waited for Chuck's direction and gently leaned into the girl's embrace. Rikki knew who she was there for, and Chuck was glad to see that the dog had forgotten about her owner's discomfort. When he saw Rikki's trademark "hug," he knew he didn't have to worry.

Chuck's mind now went to what would make the whole thing better—what he could do to help Zoe stay calm and be able to testify. And that was a good distraction from the deep ache in his ankle.

* * *

When the courthouse therapy dogs program was launched in 2007, dogs were only allowed to meet with children in the victim advocate office, the idea being to keep them out of sight as much as possible. Chuck lobbied successfully to allow the team to escort the child and their family members to the courtroom and wait outside while they went in to testify. That could be the most difficult time to manage a child's anxieties and energy levels. But dogs were not allowed in the courtroom itself.

Zoe's family gathered on the wooden benches in the corridor a little before nine a.m., when the trial was scheduled to begin. There was Danielle, her parents, her mother-in-law, her sister-in-law, and her husband's cousin. Zoe's father had purposely stayed behind the scenes throughout the ordeal. He and Danielle were trying to keep their home life as normal looking as possible for the kids' sake, so other family members stepped in for moral support.

As soon as Chuck sat down, Zoe got on the floor with Rikki, and the two were like old playmates. Although she seemed relaxed, Chuck wondered how Zoe would respond once she was in the witness chair. Would she be able to answer the attorneys' questions? That was his biggest worry—that she would see "Mr. Frank" and shut down.

During their previous visits, they hadn't had time for small talk, so Danielle started telling Chuck more about their family. As usual, the conversation turned to pets.

Danielle said they had recently adopted a rescue after visiting a Humane Society information booth. Ever since they'd met Rikki, Zoe and her six-year-old brother, Eli, had been asking their parents about getting a dog. On Valentine's Day, Zoe was twirling a baton in a parade. Eli and his father were wandering around an exhibition area and met Scooby, who had been given up by his previous owners. He was friendly and easygoing, even around the highly active Eli. Scooby looked like a pit bull and bulldog mix but ran like a greyhound, Danielle said. He had proved to be very gentle, which she said was especially important because they would have a new baby soon. She was taking Scooby to basic obedience classes and hoped that maybe one day he, too, could be a therapy dog.

During lulls in the conversation with Chuck, Danielle watched her daughter playing with Rikki, which was helping ease her concern for Zoe. She was trying not to get worked up, because she didn't want the stress to prompt her to go into premature labor. Danielle had brought a book for herself, hoping it might take her mind off of things, but when she tried reading, she just couldn't concentrate. At least Zoe was okay as long as Rikki was there.

Danielle was mentally exhausted. This drama was finally going to come to an end—for better or worse—after consuming their lives for three years. As she tried to push away anxiety about her court appearance, she was suddenly seized with a craving for a candy bar. And her expectant mommy condition required that it be a Twix or a Milky Way. When she heard there was going to be a delay in calling witnesses, Danielle saw it as an opportunity to satisfy that craving. She pushed herself up from the hard wooden bench and went on a hunt for sugar.

Because Danielle was a witness, she was barred from hearing any other testimony—including her own daughter's. So she had asked her sister-in-law, Angela, to accompany Zoe into the courtroom. Angela—along with

Danielle's parents and mother-in-law, and her husband's cousin Trisha—would be her eyes and ears.

Danielle didn't think the case would take long to try, but as the morning dragged on, she was grateful that Susan Parmalee kept providing updates. The defense was trying to convince the judge that the October hearing wasn't sufficient in determining Zoe's competency as a witness. And, though he'd had her videotaped testimony for two years, the defense attorney wanted parts of it—the ones that referred to multiple incidents—redacted before the jury saw it.

The prosecutor, John Hutchins, argued that the court had conducted an inquiry previously and had found the child competent to testify. The defense attorney, Joel Remland, had "slapped down two cases" on his desk five minutes before the trial started, saying they were going to cite them as case law to argue that the court's questioning wasn't good enough.

After giving the case law a quick review, the judge sided with Remland. That meant Zoe would need to be questioned twice—once outside of the jury's presence and once in. And the judge said she would consider how the girl responded that day in comparison to what she said at the October hearing.

Hutchins objected vigorously to the videotape redaction as well—it had already been litigated—and Remland's insistence to suppress parts of it was untimely. Remland admitted that he hadn't thought about the statements

on the videotape at the October hearing but said that
he had a new cocounsel who'd brought the references to
his attention. To give the defendant a fair trial, he felt the
judge would need to address it.

Hutchins wanted to avoid yet another rescheduling of
the trial—how could he put Zoe and her mother through
that?—so he agreed to the redacting, though he didn't
hide his frustration. He said Remland had brought the
issue up more than four months ago and had made the
decision not to file a written motion, instead waiting until
the morning of the trial, "basically sandbagging the state."

The judge dismissed Hutchins's argument and
moved on.

As Danielle heard the reports, she decided it was
becoming a circus act. Everything was last minute. She
just wanted to hurry up and get it over with.

About midmorning, Hutchins came out to tell
Danielle that she would only be asked questions to establish a time frame and geography, because Zoe was too
young to do that part. Then he told her there had been
another delay related to jury instruction. The defense was
trying to craft a specific definition for the word "vagina."

* * *

Hutchins told the judge that Zoe's mom, Danielle, was the
next witness. After she was seated in the witness chair, he
greeted her and, for the record, confirmed she was Zoe's

mother. He asked Zoe's birthdate to establish that she was five years old at the time of the incident, then asked how Danielle knew the defendant, Frank Dieter.

"He was best friends with myself and my husband at the time," she said.

"Now, you spent a lot of time hanging out with the defendant and his wife, is that correct?"

"Oh, yes."

"And you trusted him to watch your kids?"

"I did."

"You had no ill will, no bad feelings between the two of you?"

"None at all. We spent every weekend together."

"Now, I would like to direct your attention to the night of April 21 of 2007. Were you at home with your husband that night?"

"We were at home for a little while."

"Okay. Did you leave at some point that night?"

"We did. My husband and I left together to go to the grocery store, and we let Mr. Dieter babysit while we were gone." She'd put the children to bed and checked on them prior to leaving to make sure they were asleep.

"When you got home that night, did the defendant say anything to you about Zoe?"

"When I got home, he met me at the front door, as I was unloading the groceries, and let me know that Zoe had woken up and that they played a game on the computer together."

"Now, did you check on Zoe before you went to bed that night?"

"I checked on her shortly after getting all the groceries in. And she was awake at that time." She had noticed that Zoe had a very odd look on her face. A blank look, something Danielle would never forget.

"Did you think anything of it at the time?"

"I did not think anything of it at the time, because we had all had the flu [that week], very high fevers and the flu. I thought possibly she was getting what we had all had."

Hutchins asked her about attending church the next day and asked if she noticed anything about Zoe the next morning.

"She didn't seem quite herself . . . One distinct thing I've always remembered was that—again, we had been to the grocery store—she walked over to the pantry and pulled out a brand-new box of Cheerios that had never been opened and put them in the trashcan."

"Was that unusual for her?"

"We thought that was very unusual. But, you know, again, we thought she was possibly getting the flu. So we just kind of brushed it off, got ready . . . and went on to church."

It wasn't long before someone came to Danielle's adult Sunday school class, saying it was very important. "We then went to our pastor's office. And that's when they told me what [Zoe] had said, what she told Mr. Langston."

Zoe was in "Papa Wayne" Langston's Sunday school class and had been very clingy that morning. As a surrogate grandfather to Zoe, he knew she was an affectionate child, but he could tell this was different. She wanted to sit in his lap or stay by him the whole time while the other children played together. He asked her what was wrong, and she said Mr. Frank had woken her up the previous night. Langston asked why Frank had woken her up, and she said she did not know. He continued to question her, and she said Mr. Frank had told her she could not tell anyone. Papa Wayne told her they shouldn't keep secrets from each other and asked again what had happened, and she said Mr. Frank had touched her where she pee pees. After Papa Wayne told Zoe that no one has a right to touch her privates, she told him Mr. Frank had touched her where she pee pees with where he pee pees.

Langston quickly took Zoe by the hand, led her and the other children in his care to another classroom, and asked that teacher to take over, telling her there had been an emergency. He found the pastor, and together they told Danielle.

"What were you thinking when you heard this?" Hutchins asked. "I mean, what was going through your mind when you heard it?"

"I [wanted] to hurt [Frank]. I was shocked, because I trusted him. We were such good friends. We'd been friends for years. I mean . . . as couples, we spent every weekend together hanging out, playing games, going out to eat, doing stuff. And I entrusted him with my child."

Hutchins clarified, "No second thoughts at all about contacting law enforcement after your child made this statement?"

"Oh, no. No, never."

"Clearly you believed . . ." he pressed.

"I believe every word she said."

* * *

While her mother testified, Zoe twirled around Rikki near the row of benches outside the courtroom doors. Chuck thought it would be a good time to let her know that Rikki wouldn't be allowed to accompany her when she took the witness stand. Therapy dogs were not allowed in the courtrooms—*yet,* he was thinking.

Chuck had heard that the chief prosecutor was uncomfortable with the idea—he was supportive of the courthouse therapy dog program but drew the line when it came to allowing them inside the courtroom during a trial. He didn't want to give the defense teams any more ammunition to declare a mistrial or win an appeal.

Chuck was certain there were many ways to address his concerns, by putting protocols in place to cover any problems the court identified. The idea of letting dogs accompany children at such a critical time just made so much sense. The trained pet therapy teams were volunteers, so there would be little or no cost to the courts. And the therapy teams served both prosecution and defense: they would help get accurate testimony from child witnesses. Their involvement would also help the victim advocates, whose job it was to put the kids' lives back together.

Chuck was determined to identify the hurdles and then find a way around them.

* * *

After Danielle gave testimony in front of the jury, Hutchins was ready to call her daughter, the victim, to the stand.

"Any objection to that, Mr. Remland?" Judge Dempsey asked.

The defense attorney reminded the judge of a hearing he had proposed to determine eight-year-old Zoe's competency. A common strategy of defense attorneys is to disqualify as many witnesses as possible, throw out as much evidence as possible, and plant doubts about the competency and viability of anyone and anything remaining.

He would start with Zoe.

Judge Dempsey turned toward the jury. "Yes, there's an issue that I need to take up with the lawyers, ladies and gentlemen, so I'm going to have Deputy Beall escort you guys out."

The accused, Frank Dieter, remained.

Remland's request for the hearing was based on a 1988 district court of appeals case, *Griffin v. State of Florida*, which better clarified a child's role in testifying. Under common law, no child under the age of fourteen was considered competent to be a witness; however, *Griffin v. State of Florida* determined that the primary test of ability should be intelligence rather than age.

With Zoe being called in for a hearing, Prosecutor Hutchins would have to prove that his child witness had the ability to observe and recall facts and to express them in the courtroom, and that the second grader had a sense of moral obligation to tell the truth.

Remland's job was to disprove the same.

CHAPTER 9

RELEASE

Zoe entered the courtroom and found everything just like the victim advocate had told her it would be. There was the lady judge in her black robe. Mr. John, the big man with kind, gentle eyes, was behind a table directly in front of her. The man who asked her a lot of questions and made her repeat her answers was at another table on the opposite side.

He was next to Mr. Frank.

When the judge motioned toward Zoe, she walked up to the red witness chair with the microphone in front of it and sat down with her purple purse on her lap and her right arm wrapped around a stuffed cheetah she had named "Nini," a girl.

Zoe's aunt Angela took a seat on one of the pew-style benches in the gallery area directly across the room from the witness stand. The courtroom had been sealed, so it was just the attorneys, the judge, the defendant, Zoe, and her aunt.

Angela dreaded the fact that her niece was going to have to talk about what had happened—and talk about it in detail. It's what she was most nervous about. She had asked Susan Parmalee what she was allowed to do if Zoe was having a hard time while giving testimony. Basically nothing, she was told, because if Zoe was looking at her and it was even suspected that her aunt was coaching her, it could affect the trial.

At least Angela was assured that Zoe was prepared, thanks to the coloring book. And having Rikki outside of the courtroom while they waited had helped keep Zoe's mind occupied. How else do you entertain an active eight-year-old while the trial is delayed for hours?

Angela had prayed for strength to play the role of supporting family member, and it was working. But she doubted she could be as strong if she were in Danielle's shoes. Had that been her daughter, she was not sure she could have held up as well for so many years. Danielle seemed to just matter-of-factly go through it all, even when it had required taking her five-year-old daughter for a gynecology examination and sitting quietly while the defense attorney grilled Zoe during a deposition.

At least on the surface, Danielle seemed to be taking it all in stride.

Zoe settled into the witness chair.

"Hey, Zoe. How are you doing?" the judge asked.

"Good."

"I'm Judge Dempsey. Do you remember meeting me last year?"

Zoe nodded.

"Can you answer out loud?"

Zoe nodded again.

"You're shaking your head yes. Do you mean yes?"

Zoe nodded a third time.

Judge Dempsey's mommy voice took over. "You've got to say yes."

"Yes," she said quickly.

"*I* can see you shaking your head, but this lady here is writing down everything that we say. So you have to answer out loud instead of shaking your head. Okay?"

"Okay."

Following the guidelines of a competency hearing, the judge asked how old Zoe was and about her birthday. Then, when asked, Zoe gave the name of her school, her grade, and her teacher's name—both the first and last name.

Dempsey was warming her up for the tougher inquiries to come.

"I'm just going to ask you some more questions about school and stuff. And I know it's kind of weird being in a courtroom, but just try and relax as much as you can. Okay?

"What's your favorite subject?"

"Art."

"Do you have a different teacher for that or the same teacher?"

"Different."

"What's her name?"

"Mr. McDowell."

"Oh, it's a guy?"

"Yes."

"Who do you live with at your house?"

"My mom, my dad, and my brother."

Zoe couldn't remember the favorite thing she received for Christmas last year—four months ago—so the judge returned to the present moment.

"What do you have in your purse there?"

"A ball, some candy, a blue pen, a balloon."

"You've got a lot of stuff in there, huh?"

"Uh-huh."

Angela had thought Zoe would come across strong. And so far, she was proving her right. She had been worried about how the defense attorney was going to treat the child during trial. On the one hand, she knew that he would be stupid to rip into her with the jury watching. But on the other hand, she was afraid he might try to push it to the line.

But after seeing how the judge interacted with Zoe, Angela felt much better. The defense attorney would be able to do his job, but he wouldn't be allowed to just shred her—now, or later with the jury. That eased her mind a little.

"Okay. What color is your purse?"

"Purple."

"So let me ask you something. If I said that that purse was red, would that be the truth or a lie?"

"A lie."

"Have you ever seen anyone get in trouble for telling a lie?"

"Yes."

"Who was that that got in trouble? Was it you or somebody else?"

"Someone else."

"Do you remember who it was?"

"No."

"Okay. Would you get in trouble if you told a lie?"

"Yes."

"What do you think your parents would do if you lied? What kind of trouble would you get in with them if you lied to them?"

"Time-out."

"And what do they do when you go to time-out?"

"They would send me to my room."

"And you'd have to stay there for a little while?"

"Yes."

The judge asked about getting in trouble at school, and in the same economy of words, Zoe indicated she would have to sign a behavioral log.

The judge asked her, "Do you understand that if you tell a lie here in the courtroom, you could get in trouble?"

"Yes."

"And do you understand that it's important to tell the truth here in the courtroom?"

"Yes."

Dempsey turned to the prosecuting attorney and asked if he had any follow-up questions. "Based on the state's argument, no, I don't," Hutchins said. "I think the child has established that she has a moral sense of obligation to tell the truth, and I don't have any further questions for her."

Judge Dempsey turned to Remland and asked the same.

"Yes, Your Honor," Remland said, and started in. "Zoe, do you know where you are right now?"

"Yes."

"Where are you?"

"In the courtroom."

"Do you know what happens in courtrooms?"

"No."

"Do you know what an oath is?"

"Yes."

"What's an oath?"

"It's when you promise to tell the truth or promise to do something."

"Why is it important to tell the truth in court?"

"I don't know."

He pressed her: "You don't know *why* it's important to tell the truth in court?"

"No."

"What would happen if you did not tell the truth in court?"

"I would get in *big* trouble," she said.

"What else would happen if you said something in court that wasn't true—to someone else?"

"I don't know."

"If you don't tell the truth in court, could something bad happen to somebody?"

Hutchins stood up. "Judge, I'm going to object to that question. I mean, she's already established that she would get into trouble. I mean, to ask her what the consequences of basically coming to court and not telling the truth to someone else is—I think that goes beyond what she has to know or to be able to testify about."

Dempsey allowed that it might be beyond the findings they needed but said she was going to let Remland continue.

Hutchins continued, "Judge, I would ask that he rephrase that question because the way it's asked, I just think is very complicated—what would happen to *someone* else. *Who* else? Could he be more specific?"

Dempsey turned to Remland. "If you can maybe rephrase it in words that she may be able to better understand."

Remland turned back to Zoe. "If somebody lies in court, what would happen to somebody else?"

"He would go to jail or get in trouble."

"How do you feel about that?"

Hutchins broke in. "Judge, objection! That's not relevant at all."

Dempsey allowed it, anyway.

Remland repeated, "How do you feel about that, Zoe?"

"Scared."

Angela didn't envy someone who had Joel Remland's job. She couldn't fathom being an attorney who had to represent someone like Frank Dieter. *Do you really believe your client, or do you not?* she wondered. But how could you defend him if you believed he was guilty? What he was accused of doing was really serious and repulsive.

On the other hand, Angela liked Prosecutor Hutchins from the beginning. Once she got over his football-player size, that is. She wondered how this giant African American guy and little fair-skinned, freckle-faced Zoe would fit—was he going to have a big, booming voice? Instead, she saw that he always stooped down to Zoe's level, and his tone was friendly. His eyes were not overly expressive as much as they were calming. Just big and warm.

"Let me ask you this," Remland continued. "When this thing happened with you and Mr. Frank—something happened—when did that happen?"

"I don't know."

"How long ago did it happen?"

Hutchins interrupted before Zoe could answer. "Judge, I'm going to object. If he's asking her for a specific date—again . . . I think this is beyond what the court is required to make a finding for."

"At this point, I'm going to overrule the objection," Dempsey said. She looked at Remland. "I don't want to get into a long drawn-out thing about the facts of the case, but you can ask her a couple of questions about it."

"I'm trying to see if she can narrate to some extent, Judge, like what . . ."

He turned toward the witness. "Zoe, are you okay?"

"Yes."

"First of all, do you recall what year it was that something happened between you and Mr. Frank?"

"No."

"Do you know how many years ago it was?"

Hutchins stood again. "Objection. Same question."

"I'm not asking for a specific date," Remland countered.

"Overruled."

"Do you know how many years ago it was?"

"No."

"Do you know how old you were at the time something happened with you and Mr. Frank—the last time?"

"Five."

"Were you in school?"

"Yes."

"What school did you go to?"

"Wee Care."

"Do you remember any teachers you had back then?"

"Ms. Dottie."

"Where did . . . where did it happen?"

Annoyed, Hutchins said, "Judge, I'm going to *object.*" Dempsey ignored his protest.

Remland continued. "The last time it happened, where did it happen? On April 21 of 2007, where did the incident with Mr. Frank take place? Where?"

"I don't know."

Reminding Zoe of a forensics interview conducted two days after the incident, he asked if she remembered going to a place with a lady who let her play with clay and talk about what Frank Dieter had done.

"Yes."

"What happened there? What did she ask you about there?"

"What he did to me and what I don't like about it and what I do like about it."

"And where did the event take place? Where did the things take place that she asked you about?"

"I don't understand that question."

"What happened—were you being babysitted?"

"Yes."

TOP: Sickly and sluggish at first, Rikki re-gained her health and eventually won the affections of her big brother, Roscoe.

BOTTOM: Rikki has a playful side, but she's not the party girl like many others in her breed. Chuck and Patty find her affectionate, wise, and pensive.

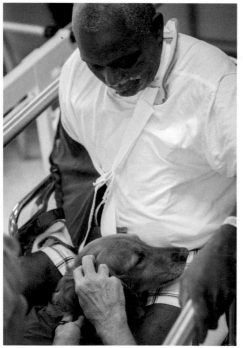

ABOVE: One of the gifts that people marvel about is Rikki's gentleness around children. She's amazingly relaxed and absorbs people's stress.

LEFT: Because of Rikki's passiveness, she had a very different calling. She seems at home in the hospital rehab and pediatric specialty units. (Photo credit: Dave Barfield)

ABOVE: Chuck Mitchell traded in his business partnerships for an entirely different one, as the human member of a therapy dog team.

LEFT: The courthouse therapy dog program sounded like a good fit for Rikki, and Chuck hoped he would be up for the challenge as well. (Photo credit: Wade Bishop, Pets Ad Litem)

ABOVE: Only a few minutes after meeting Rikki, Zoe had mastered the "kiss" trick, holding a baby carrot between her teeth as the dog gently retrieved it.

BELOW: Florida State Hospital "three stooges" and their owners. From left: Chuck Mitchell with Rikki, Allie and Melanie Howe with Great Dane Grendel, and Judy Sutton with retired show dog Caja.

ABOVE: Kids and adults alike marvel at what Rikki will do for an organic baby carrot treat.

BELOW: READ was the first comprehensive literacy support program built around the idea of having children read to dogs. Rikki became a READ canine in 2009.

ABOVE: Patty was first paired with Roscoe as a READ team in the schools, but he became fidgety at times. Rikki seemed a better fit, so Roscoe retired.

BELOW: Betsy Duval suffered a brain injury in an auto accident and wasn't expected to recover, until Rikki padded into her life. She credits the dog's near daily visits in her "coming back."

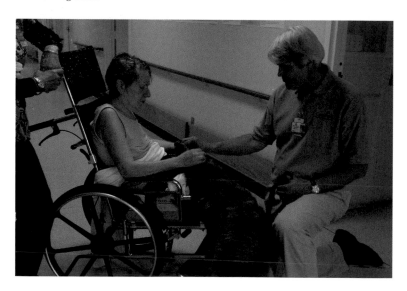

OPPOSITE, TOP: Rikki's regular weekly schedule includes the TMH Rehabilitation Center every Thursday, where therapists often request her assistance with patients. (Photo credit: Dave Barfield)

OPPOSITE, BOTTOM: Zoe and her family moved away, but met with Rikki during a return visit. The child told Chuck, "I may never be here again, but I will always remember Rikki."

LEFT: A twelve-year-old Zoe is reunited with Rikki. Her expression says it all: peace, thanksgiving. You got me through it all.

BELOW: The TMH Animal Therapy program now has an official "swearing in" ceremony for canines. Rikki was among the first to offer a paw print.

"Were you in a house?"

"I was at my house."

"Where was your mommy?"

"They were out buying groceries."

"How do you know that?"

"My mommy told me."

Remland was trying to show that Zoe had been coached by a parent. "*When* did she tell you that?"

"Before she left. She told me that we were—that her and daddy were going to go get some groceries."

"And then what happened after that?"

Hutchins jumped in. "Judge, I'm going to object. I think this child has already testified, and I don't want her to have to run through her entire direct and then have to do it again in front of the jury."

"I'm going to sustain the objection, because I think we're—"

Remland cut her off: "No further questions."

"—getting a little too far into the facts. Mr. Remland, anything else you wanted to tell me or any argument you want to make about the competency issue?"

"One second," he said. "Your Honor, I would ask that the child be taken out during argument."

Dempsey turned to Zoe. "We're going to ask that you step out of the courtroom for a couple of minutes, Zoe. Go ahead and take your stuff and we'll be back with you."

Angela was already standing up, ready to get Zoe out of there. She grabbed her hand as the bailiff led her through the little gate. Barely outside the door, Zoe dropped her aunt's hand and raced past her waiting mother and grandmother, then threw her entire body across Rikki, who was asleep at Chuck's feet. Unalarmed by the suddenness of Zoe's approach, Rikki continued to lie still, as if absorbing the child's stress.

Taking a seat next to Danielle, Angela reassured her about what happened in the courtroom. She couldn't believe how strong Zoe had come across. She had known the child would do well; she just had never thought she would do *that* well.

Angela told Danielle that Zoe did not even hesitate with her answers; she was attentive and confident. "She finally stopped nodding her head and got the yeses and nos down," she said. "Zoe was very brave."

* * *

With Zoe out of the courtroom, Remland started his argument to get the child disqualified as a witness. It was the third time he had been allowed to question her—the first time in deposition and the second in a hearing—and he knew the effect Zoe's presence would have on a jury. At one point, he had even remarked to a victim advocate how beautiful and well behaved she was. "I could take this child home with me," he said.

But a man's life was on the line, so he started in. "On the three bases on *Griffin* [and a second case, *J. B. J. v.*

State of Florida], I think that the state's case for competency here is not met . . . I don't think that she meets the requirements as far as the moral obligation to tell the truth. I mean, I think she can tell the difference between a truth and a lie, but that's not sufficient. I think that she understands that . . . she might be sent for time-out, she might get in trouble for lying. But I think that's as far as it goes. I don't think there's any clear evidence that she understands the moral obligation to tell the truth in a court of law as far as, you know, what would happen if she lied and why she should tell the truth and that type of thing. So I think that's insufficient.

"As far as the ability to recollect the facts, there's a lot of 'I-don't-knows.' I'm not sure that's sufficient here. There seems to be a lack of evidence in that regard, Judge. She's very vague . . .

"As far as narrating or describing what occurred, we didn't go through probably that much on direct. We did go through a little bit, but I think she's deficient in that area as well. So I would just ask the court to apply the case law to what you've heard today and find that she's not competent."

Judge Dempsey acknowledged Remland's discourse. "Okay. Thank you. Mr. Hutchins?"

After ten years of prosecuting for the state, it still amazed John Hutchins to hear the kind of baloney defense attorneys use to discredit a witness.

He took a deep breath and began, "Judge, in the case law that's been presented by the defense this morning, *State versus Griffin*, there's basically three things: Whether the child is capable of observing and recollecting facts. The child has been able to testify this morning that she was in . . . pre-K. She was able to recall her teacher from three years ago. She was able to tell you who her teacher is now. She's able to tell you who she stays with. She's able to tell you who her art teacher is—who is different than her regular teacher. I think it's clear the child is able to recall facts, and she is able to testify.

"Whether the child is capable of narrating those facts to the court or to the jury—well, Judge, you had an opportunity to see the [forensics interview video], as well as the hearing that we held in October as well as the hearing we've had today. Clearly, Judge, the child is able to tell what has happened to her, and she's able to recall the facts of the abuse, and she's able to relay those. And she should be allowed to do that here in court today.

"Mr. Remland started by saying that the child has no moral sense of an obligation to tell the truth. Well, I disagree, Judge. She stated very clearly on the stand that if she tells a lie, she gets into *big* trouble. She stated that there are consequences for it—that she could end up in time-out. She clearly knows the difference between the truth and a lie and . . . that she has to tell the truth here today. And I'll even take it a step further. Mr. Remland asked the child if she knew what an oath was. And she went on to say that it means you tell the truth or if you say you're going to do something, then you do it.

"Clearly, this child has a moral sense of the obligation to tell the truth.

"I think the state has more than met its burden, Judge. . . . This is an articulate, precocious child. The court was able to ask her about what she had in her purse and, without even looking, she was able to recall I want to say at least five or six different items that were in her purse.

"So, based on all of that, Judge, we would ask the court to deny the defendant's motion and basically find the child competent to testify."

It was Judge Dempsey's turn. "Okay. So focusing on the three considerations that really all the cases talk about . . . [Zoe] was able to tell us her age, her date of birth, who she lived with, where she went to school, her teacher's name, her favorite subject—which was art—and the teacher that taught that class. She described all the contents of her purple purse without going through [it]. . . .

"She remembered the name of the school or pre-school that she went to when she was five and her teacher's name, Ms. Dottie, that she had at that school. She was able to provide an intelligent definition of what an oath is—which I doubt many eight-year-olds can do. She also provided some details about the incident itself. . . . I'm going to find that she's clearly capable of observing and recollecting facts and narrating those facts to the court.

"Regarding the issue of a moral sense of obligation to tell the truth, she testified that she had seen people get in trouble before for telling a lie and that she could get in trouble for telling a lie with both her mom or at school. At home, she would be given a time-out. At school, she might be required to sign a behavior log, which I'm familiar with through my own kids. . . . She clearly understood that she could get in trouble for telling a lie in court . . . And . . . she seems like a very intelligent and just very composed eight-year-old, just from being able to observe her last October as well as today. So I'm going to find that she clearly is competent to testify.

"Anything else before we bring the jury back in?"

Remland reasserted his objection about the competency, and Judge Dempsey acknowledged it. "Let's bring the jury back in—and I guess if you want to, get [Zoe]."

The bailiff called for the girl, who was sitting on the ground next to Rikki. Angela got her attention and said the judge needed her again. Zoe turned to Chuck and pleaded with him. "Please, can Rikki come into the courtroom with me, *please*?"

Chuck told her that Rikki would be right here waiting for her as soon as she got out, like last time. And he pulled out one of Rikki's business cards—the one with her in the blue bandana—and said, "When you have a hard time, be sure to look at [this picture] of Rikki and remember we're just behind the door waiting for you." He said he would save some carrots for her, too.

Zoe gave Rikki a long hug, and as Chuck's throat clenched he thought, *I will do everything in my power to avoid ever having to tell a child again that the dog can't go with them in the courtroom.*

He looked down, and Rikki was looking right into his eyes with what he read as distress. *What is the matter?* her eyes said. *Why aren't you letting me do my job? I can feel it, she needs me!*

As Zoe pulled away, he whispered to Rikki, "Don't worry, sweetheart. We will make this right." And his mind turned to devising a strategy to prevent children from ever being denied a therapy dog when they needed her most.

The judge motioned for Zoe to sit in the red chair again, and after the jury was seated, John Hutchins greeted her. When the judge asked her to spell her name for the nice court reporter and to introduce herself to the members of the jury, she said, "Z-o-e, I'm Zoe." She also spelled her last name. When asked, she gave her age, her birthdate, and the name of her neighborhood. She told the jury her brother's age, the name of her teacher, and her favorite subject at school. Hutchins then asked if she knew "somebody by the name of Mr. Frank." Zoe confirmed he was friends with her mom and told how he came into her bedroom one night while babysitting and woke her up. He told her not to tell anybody. She said, "He sticked his pee in my pee." He "slobbered" on his finger and put that inside of her first.

Hutchins had to prove penetration for both charges, so he used a cup and a pencil to demonstrate that Zoe knew the difference between being outside and inside.

She recalled eventually telling Papa Wayne at Sunday school what had happened, and when Hutchins showed her the anatomical drawings from the forensics interview, she confirmed the body parts involved.

Finally, Hutchins asked, "Zoe, do you see the person here in court today that touched you with his hand and also with his pee-pee?" She said yes and pointed to Mr. Frank.

Defense Attorney Joel Remland declined to cross-examine the witness.

When Judge Dempsey said that Zoe was free to go, she walked quickly across the courtroom. Once outside the door, she raced toward Rikki, wrapping her whole body around the dog. She asked Chuck for carrots but started feeding them to the dog so quickly that Chuck had to ask her to slow down. She was a bundle of nerves.

The team stayed a little while longer, but when Chuck heard that Zoe was leaving with her grandmother, he and Rikki said their good-byes. Danielle and the rest of the family members remained, even as the trial dragged on through the evening. Redacting the videotape wasn't as easy as it sounded, and jurors had to hear from the nurse who conducted Zoe's physical examination, the forensics interviewer, a crime laboratory DNA expert, and a deputy sheriff. Jurors also heard the audiotape of a call Frank

Dieter made to the sheriff's office a few days after the incident, when he admitted to "touching" a five-year-old girl. He talked about having a guilt complex and speculating that he was going to go to jail for five or ten years. "I have no idea why I touched this little girl . . . I just don't know. I did it. I got caught."

After hearing closing arguments by the attorneys, jurors were excused for deliberation, and two hours later, they had their verdict. Susan called Chuck around ten thirty p.m. with the news: the jury had found Frank Dieter guilty on all counts. Because both were capital crimes, Florida's mandatory minimum sentencing law applied. He would be serving two life sentences without the possibility of parole.

CHAPTER 10

LAW DOG

With Zoe's trial behind him, Chuck was able to take the next step his doctors were recommending: surgery to replace his ankle. It had been almost a year since his injury, and two reconstructive surgeries had failed. The other procedures had only limited his mobility, but replacement meant he and Rikki would not be working together as a team for at least three months.

Danielle and Susan kept Chuck informed about other developments related to the case through e-mail. There was still a formal hearing ahead for Frank Dieter to receive his sentence, even though there was only one penalty the judge could impose according to Florida law: life without parole.

Danielle, now thirty-nine weeks pregnant, insisted on attending the sentencing. It was held in the same courtroom as the trial, and she was seated on one of the long wooden benches in the gallery. She looked over at Frank: he didn't look nearly as good as he had only eight days before at the trial. This time he was dressed in jail scrubs and was unshaven—kind of scruffy looking, she thought.

Defense Attorney Joel Remland had filed a motion for a new trial, reiterating arguments he had used previously, but Judge Dempsey had denied it. Prosecutor Hutchins then told the judge that there was a witness who wanted to address the court, and handed her a drawing on behalf of the victim, Zoe.

Danielle stood up. She said she wanted to explain the illustration, since her daughter was not there to narrate it. At the top, Zoe had written, "Dear Judge, I felt scared when Mr. Frank did what he did. I want him to go to jail forever and ever. I don't want him to hurt other kids."

The drawing depicted people with titles below: a lawyer (smiling), a judge (in her black robe, smiling), Zoe (portrayed with a squiggly mouth and a frightened look in her eyes), and the jury (a blue glob in the corner).

Danielle had also prepared a personal statement explaining how everything had influenced her family. She began. "Ever since the day [Zoe] told, our lives have changed. I had entrusted the two most important things in my life to my best friend, to someone I greatly trusted, and that [trust] was broken beyond repair. It has not only affected the trust between me and him but trust for all people.

"I have a very hard time trusting anyone, especially with my children. When I leave them at church or even school, or they go to a friend's house to play, I worry what might happen when I'm not watching. If someone close to me, who had gained so much trust with me over eight years of friendship, someone who had watched my baby girl grow up—how could they do something like he did? How am I to trust anyone else?"

She said there was also the loss of best friends, the people she regarded as her only true friends. "We spent every weekend possible with Mr. Dieter and his wife, and now we have no friends to hang out with and confide in. His wife and I were best friends, and now that friendship is tarnished forever.

"They were not able to have children, and I thought he was loving mine like his own . . ." She paused, then continued, "I spent a lot of time being angry with him and am still very hurt, but my hope and prayer is that he will find Jesus and change his ways. Without my faith in God, I don't know that I would be standing here today."

In raising her daughter, Danielle said she now second-guessed everything. When Zoe exhibited certain behaviors, she couldn't help but wonder, *Is this normal, or is it because of what he did to her, taking her innocence from her at such a young age?*

She concluded her statement. "[Zoe] is a tough little girl, and I know that with God by our side we will make it through this. But every day for the rest of her life and the rest of our lives, we will live with this. We . . . have and we will move on with our lives, but it will always be there . . . therefore, I only feel it is right that [Frank] spend every day of his life paying for the consequence of what he did."

The judge thanked Danielle and confirmed with Hutchins the prescribed life sentence, then gave Defense Attorney Remland an opportunity to respond. He said that Frank Dieter had a right to make a statement but had declined, then turned to Dieter, who made an inaudible response. Remland turned back to the judge. "He doesn't have anything to say. It's a mandatory life sentence. And I have advised him of his right to appeal, as [he] will do, I'm sure."

Judge Dempsey quickly confirmed that she adjudicated Dieter "guilty" and assigned him the expected sentence: life without the possibility of parole on both counts. "Although it might not matter," she added, "I'm going to give you credit for the time you have served." The clerk volunteered the number: 1,084 days. The judge also designated him as a "sexual predator" and ordered a DNA sample.

With sentencing concluded, the judge asked the attorneys about details for the trial involving charges against Dieter on behalf of a second victim, Brady. Danielle remembered seeing the beautiful dark-skinned teenager at an earlier hearing when they were considering trying Zoe's case and Brady's together. Rikki had played a key role in comforting both girls that day. The judge determined that Dieter would face charges involving Brady the following July.

Prosecutor Hutchins went to work building that case next. Seventeen-year-old Brady had gone for her first gynecology exam after some cysts had formed on her ovaries. She insisted that her mother, Tonya, be in the room for the exam and Pap smear, then became so emotional during the procedure that even the doctor was stunned.

Two days later, Brady didn't come home from her part-time job. Tonya called the sheriff's office and reported her as a runaway. When Brady returned the next day, she revealed the secret she had been keeping from her mother for ten years.

"Remember when you used to drop me and Bianca off at Mr. Frank and Ms. Heather's house while you traveled?

"Well, there was this one Sunday—I remember because I was wearing that black zip-up dress that I was just obsessed with. You were on one of your business trips, so we were spending the night. Mr. Frank put Bianca to bed, but I wasn't sleepy. So he asked if I wanted him to read me a book. I was about eight years old; he told me to sit in his lap. About halfway through the book, he started rubbing my leg. And then he went through my underwear.

"I got up and said I just wanted to go to bed. He said he wasn't hurting me. Then he made me put my hands on the top of his pants. I went into the room with Bianca, and he followed me. He asked if I wanted him to tuck me in. I said no, I just wanted to go to sleep.

"I remember just holding Bianca all night. I didn't go to sleep; I was just holding her.

"The next morning, I was in the kitchen eating cereal. His wife was in the house. He told me not to tell anybody and that he didn't hurt me.

"Mama, you probably don't remember this, but whenever you asked about us staying over there, I would say no. I didn't tell you why. I just never wanted to go over there again."

Tonya recalled the relationship. She had sold Tupperware with Frank Dieter's wife. The couple didn't have children of their own and seemed to love having her kids around. Tonya was new to town, separated from Brady's father, and being a single parent was difficult. So when the Dieters offered to take the kids to church with them on Sundays and occasionally keep them overnight, Tonya didn't find it peculiar. They seemed so nice.

Tonya called the sheriff's office again and told them her runaway daughter had returned, but she needed to file a second report. She gave the whole story, and when the deputy asked if she knew Frank Dieter's whereabouts, she said no. The incident report was filed: "Lewd/lascivious molestation—offender 18 or older against victim less than 12 years old." The suspect's whereabouts: at large.

When violent crimes detective Todd Chaires, the lead on Zoe's case, received the report, he couldn't believe the coincidence. Dieter's abuse of Zoe had not been publicized, so there was no way Brady could have known he was already being held in the county jail. It was what cops call "dumb criminal luck."

But Brady still needed to be interviewed by the child protection team and to identify Dieter in a photo lineup. Chaires waited until they had a warrant for Dieter's arrest, served at the Leon County Jail where he was incarcerated, before contacting the state attorney's office.

It had been ten years since Brady had seen the man she knew as Mr. Frank, but seconds after the six male Caucasian faces were presented in the photo lineup, she pointed to Dieter. And in the forensics interview with Kimberly Ellis, who had also interviewed Zoe, she recalled enough details to confirm the charge: capital sexual battery on a child under the age of twelve.

The Sixth Amendment to the United States Constitution contains a protection for the accused that can be agonizing for victims. Called the "confrontation clause," it states that a person accused of a crime "shall enjoy the right . . . to be confronted with the witnesses against him." Over the years, case law had challenged that right when the witnesses were child victims, but in Dieter's case, Zoe and Brady were not exempt.

The first time the girls saw Mr. Frank again was during a hearing that took place a year after Brady had come forward and two and a half years after he had babysat Zoe. Held in a courtroom, it had all the formality of a trial but without a jury. There were several critical things to be determined: whether there were enough similarities in the two victims' cases to have one trial, whether Zoe was a competent witness, the reliability of the DNA taken from Zoe's sheets, and whether videotaped interviews with the victims would be admissible.

Knowing the experience would be difficult for both girls, Susan Parmalee arranged to have Chuck and Rikki available to them. The tension is fairly constant in a courthouse, but it always seemed to dissipate when a therapy team showed up. Smiles broke out and anxieties melted away. Chuck noticed it as he trailed the tail-swaying Rikki toward the meeting place; he felt a little like Santa Claus.

The waiting area outside of courtroom 3B consisted of a bank of elevators and rows of benches divided by an atrium. Not knowing in what order the attorneys were calling witnesses for the hearing, everyone, from the DNA crime lab analyst and forensics interviewer to the victims and their family members, was arranged along the walls.

Rikki had assigned herself to Zoe.

The defense had filed a motion to exclude the DNA samples in Zoe's case, and Defense Attorney Remland's expert was located out of state. There were technical difficulties with the speakerphone, which caused delays, and the hearing dragged on until late afternoon, requiring both the victims and many witnesses to wait.

Rikki lay down and fell asleep in Zoe's lap—something she doesn't normally do—and Chuck wasn't quite sure who was comforting whom.

Brady was the first victim called, and Chuck watched as this poised and confident young adult suddenly metamorphosed into a scared little girl. When she came out of the courtroom sobbing and shaking only a few minutes later, her father was physically supporting her. Chuck saw a look of despair on the man's face, combined with the kind of rage that only a father could feel.

Rikki's head popped up and she paused, as if assessing the situation. Slowly, she stood up and started moving toward Brady. Chuck had not been introduced to the girl previously, although he knew there was a second victim, so he followed Rikki's lead cautiously. *She may not even like dogs,* he thought. But as usual, Chuck's partner knew what to do. She gently extended her head and touched Brady's hand; the girl responded by stroking Rikki's ears.

Two other trials were ending, and the halls started filling up. Prosecutor Hutchins told Brady she was done for the day, so Chuck and Rikki moved back over to Zoe. Judge John Cooper, who had been one of Chuck's attorneys when he sued Walmart, saw them in the hallway and came over. He stood watching the child petting and hugging Rikki, and Danielle told him how much the dog had helped their family.

Judge Terry Lewis, another acquaintance of Chuck's, also came to say hello. When he heard about the work

Rikki was doing, he said the trial they had just finished was similar, and he thought a therapy dog would have made a difference for that victim as well.

* * *

Four days after Frank Dieter's sentencing hearing, Danielle gave birth to a healthy baby boy. She and her family were trying to put everything behind them, but news trickled in occasionally. She heard that Remland had filed an appeal based on pretrial competency-of-witness rulings, sufficiency of evidence, and jury instruction. The nightmare just would not go away.

But she also heard that two weeks before the trial date for Brady, Dieter's defense accepted a plea of fifteen years, which would run concurrent with the life sentence. She couldn't help but recall the judge's comment at sentencing: *Not that it mattered.*

* * *

While sidelined with ankle-replacement surgery and rehab, Chuck took on a new project: finding solutions that would allow therapy dogs in the courtroom. He decided his best chance would be to convince the state attorney, Willie Meggs, to allow it. In addition to being a former US marine, cop, and deputy, in his spare time Meggs was an active member of the Gideons, an evangelical Christian organization that provides Bibles for hotel rooms. He was known for being tough, and his wiry frame matched his reputation as a strong protector of the courts.

Chuck had been told that Meggs's initial reaction to the idea of using therapy dogs to comfort child victims in the courthouse building wasn't exactly warm and fuzzy. "You want to do *what*? You want to bring dogs into *what*?" But he was an animal lover—he owned a horse and a mule—so ultimately the proponents won him over. And once the courthouse therapy dogs program was up and running, he even received a little shine at the National District Attorneys Association meeting for being a trendsetter. Meggs found that amusing.

But now that he was hearing rumors about dogs going into the courtroom itself, he was drawing the line: "Dogs in my courtroom? They'll run me out of town!"

Victim advocates understood his concern. The prosecution's worst-case scenario was to have a conviction overturned, thus setting a child molester free, or to have to do a trial all over again two or three years later following a successful appeal, thus dragging a child back through it all. The prosecutors who tried these cases really cared about the kids and their families. Sure, they wanted justice, but if a child could be spared the trauma, that was their preference.

Chuck did some homework. He knew that Meggs and the local sheriff, Larry Campbell, were friends and that Campbell was supportive of animal therapy, so he invited the two to lunch. That's when Meggs laid it out for him. "Here's the problem. There's been no case law." Meggs had checked, and there was nothing that he could find that gave him confidence one way or the other. "And if I lose a conviction because I have a dog in the courtroom . . ."

Chuck already had a counterargument prepared. "Can we at least develop some protocols? I mean, these kids can't talk—they're freezing up."

Meggs wasn't buying it.

A skilled negotiator in business, Chuck had been at this type of intersection before. "So what have I got to do? What would make all the concerns go away?"

Jokingly, Meggs said, "Well, if there was a law, it would be different."

"So, if I wrote a law . . ."

Meggs shrugged. "I'd have to allow it."

Chuck could hardly wait to get back to his computer that day. It was early fall, so there was still time to build support and file a law before the Florida legislature met the following spring. He knew he couldn't do this on sheer volunteer effort, though. Chuck hired a lobbyist (who ultimately donated his time) and called in a few favors from other dog-friendly types who worked in the legislature. He even lined up Danielle to give testimony, if needed. There were support letters from victim advocates as well.

From the following March through early May, Chuck attended every legislative gathering where the issue might be heard. Then they got lucky: Florida had some

high-profile cases involving sexual predators, and the
Walk in Their Shoes Act was being considered to further
crack down on the trend. The law that Rikki and Zoe had
inspired could easily be added as an amendment. In the
fourteen-page act related to sexual offenses, lawmakers
inserted a paragraph that stated:

> *[In] judicial or other proceedings involving victim
> or witness under the age of 16 or person with men-
> tal retardation; special protections; use of registered
> service or therapy animals . . . the court may set any
> other conditions it finds just and appropriate on the
> taking of testimony by a child, including the use of
> a service or therapy animal that has been evalu-
> ated and registered according to national standards,
> in any proceeding involving a sexual offense. When
> deciding whether to permit a child to testify with the
> assistance of a registered service or therapy animal,
> the court shall take into consideration the age of the
> child, the interests of the child, the rights of the parties
> to the litigation, and any other relevant factor that
> would facilitate the testimony by the child.*

After twenty-five individual legislative actions over
five months, including seven formal votes by various
committees and subcommittees, the Walk in Their Shoes
Act had no dissenting votes in the house or the senate—a
rare occurrence in lawmaking. It was approved by the

governor, and on July 1, 2011, Florida became the first state in the nation to allow dogs in the courtroom.

To celebrate the victory, Chuck and Patty invited Zoe, Danielle, her husband, and leaders of the courthouse therapy dog program to a dinner with the lobbyists. Adding to the festive mood was a personal victory that came on the same day. After more than a year of reviewing nine volumes of court documents, testimony, and physical evidence, three appellate judges in the First District Court of Appeal affirmed the lower court's decision in *State of Florida v. Frank Dieter* using three words: "Per curiam. Affirmed." It meant that Dieter would be incarcerated for the rest of his natural life.

Danielle and her husband shared another bit of news at the dinner. Their family had an opportunity to return to Kentucky, where they had lived previously. They hoped it would provide a fresh start for all of them—most especially Zoe. They promised to stay in touch.

Later in the fall, on a return trip to Tallahassee, Danielle contacted Chuck to see if they could visit with Rikki. She said Zoe kept a photo of the dog in her bedroom and still talked about her as she would about a childhood friend.

Danielle told him, "I don't think Zoe could have testified without Rikki. I don't think Zoe could have done the deposition without her, and I just don't think Zoe would be doing as well now without Rikki, because that was her comfort, that was her friend. That was the positive amongst all the negatives." Danielle said her daughter looks back on the experience and only thinks of Rikki. She doesn't think about the bad stuff that happened.

"She knew if she was going to the courthouse, Rikki was going to be there. That helped. There was always something to look forward to. Instead of 'I've got to go talk about this again,' it was 'We're going to see Rikki. I've got to have carrots.'"

Chuck and Danielle set a date and time to meet at a city park. As soon as the family van pulled up and the now nine-year-old Zoe spotted Rikki, she was reaching for the door. Her middle brother, Eli, was with them, so they took turns feeding Rikki carrots and practicing the "kiss" trick. When Danielle, Eli, and her new baby brother moved over to the monkey bars, Zoe sat on the curb next to Chuck and Rikki. They both stroked the dog's fur, and Zoe whispered something in Rikki's ear. Then she told Chuck, "I may never be here again, but I will always remember Rikki."

CHAPTER 11

CLINICAL ASSIST

Three days before Christmas 2011, Rikki and Chuck arrived to make rounds in the Tallahassee Memorial Rehabilitation Center. The nurses' station was draped in Christmas lights, and therapists were garbed in their snowflake and reindeer print scrubs. Patients and visitors were taking turns playing Christmas carols on the piano in the reception area, while Rikki, in her multicolored paw print bandana (she wasn't big on Santa hats), added to the festive mood.

In the downstairs gym, patients were seated and waiting for therapists to guide their workout. A woman with a zipper-like scar on her leg was making pedaling motions on a mini cycle machine, while a pale-faced man using a walker moved across the room with an oxygen tank trailing behind him.

As soon as Chuck and Rikki turned the corner, one of the patients said, "There's that beautiful dog I've heard so much about." Rikki slowly moved toward the zipper-leg lady and nuzzled her while the other patients watched and patiently waited their turn. Thursday mornings were "Rikki days," and some therapists told their patients about this "magic dog" that often visited to help them work.

After an hour of alternating between patient workstations in both gyms, Chuck and Rikki stopped by Sheree Porter's office. The program manager for rehab, Sheree had been key to expanding animal-assisted therapy (AAT) in medical environments, and Chuck wanted to tell her about some progress he'd made on clinical trials to measure AAT's effect on patients. He had initiated discussions between the Florida State University College of Medicine and Tallahassee Memorial Hospital to conduct a study comparing patients who used animal therapy to those who did not. He hoped the studies would explain the biochemistry of what happens in a person's body and provide details through the patient's self-assessment after an AAT session. Chuck had also proposed combining the trial with veterinary medicine to measure the stress hormones in the therapy dogs. After observing Rikki's energy level following visits, he suspected that it wasn't easy work.

Sheree, a "dog person," greeted Rikki like an old friend. After quickly catching up on new developments with Chuck, she asked if he and Rikki had time to visit a patient with severe traumatic brain injury (TBI). By all means, he said. Chuck knew a little bit about TBI from a brief encounter with a woman in the hospital's intensive care unit. That was the first time he had witnessed the effects of Rikki's interaction by observing a heart rate and blood pressure monitor. It was one thing to read the studies of the positive effects of pet therapy interactions and to see it on the faces of those they visited. But he received a real charge seeing it confirmed by technology.

This TBI case was much more serious, it seemed. Betsy Duval, sixty-seven, of Sarasota, had been visiting her sister in Tallahassee in early November when their car was T-boned by a truck on a rural road. Duval's sister Margie had also required rehabilitation for her broken bones, but Betsy's injuries were life threatening. She was in a deep coma initially, and doctors were not certain she would ever recover. It had been about six weeks, but they still weren't sure if she would ever again master the basic skills of chewing, swallowing, and speaking coherently.

To explain a TBI patient's behaviors to family members, Sheree often used a filing cabinet analogy. From birth, we begin to collect everything we see, smell, learn, and so forth, and put it into the correct "file." Everything's well organized in the drawer, and you know where it is. But when a person suffers a traumatic brain injury, it's like someone dumped the contents of that file drawer on the floor, then scooped it all up and put it back into the cabinet in no particular order.

With a brain injury, the information is probably still there in the filing cabinet, but you don't know where to find it. So going through rehabilitation—the cognitive retraining—is like getting your file folders back in order. As the folders containing skills that move our bodies through the routines of life are being re-sorted, there's no predicting the patient's behavior or responses.

Sheree explained some of the unique requirements of working with a TBI patient. She asked Chuck not to speak unless necessary. Part of the plan for Betsy's therapy was to isolate the senses by controlling stimulation. For example, if a person was speaking, they shouldn't be touching the patient. If touching, they shouldn't be speaking. Lights were kept off in the room, as that was one of the strongest forms of stimulation.

When Chuck and Rikki entered Betsy's room, only a small amount of filtered light was coming from the window. The patient's bed was covered in what looked like a seine net, which was tightly zipped. Chuck learned later that this was used to keep her from falling out of bed during a seizure. Betsy was wearing a neck brace that added sternness to her appearance; she was hooked up to feeding tubes, and her eyes were shut, even though her body seemed wide awake with movement.

Sheree spoke quietly. "Betsy, I brought a dog here to see you today." Sheree then motioned for Chuck and Rikki to get on the side of the bed closest to the window, since there was a wall of equipment on the opposite side.

Chuck saw a woman with a thin frame, who he guessed was in her mid to late sixties. Her arms and legs were thrashing, threatening to disconnect the tubes coming out of all parts of her body. Chuck wanted to get Rikki's head up to where Betsy could touch it, but the bed was higher than Rikki could reach. He dug into his pocket for a carrot and lured the dog closer, then held her there until the woman's arm fell across Rikki's head. Sheree helped by taking Betsy's arm and rubbing it across Rikki's nose and ears.

All of a sudden, Betsy yelled, "Dog!" and after a few strokes more, "Golden!" Sheree wondered how in the world she had identified Rikki's breed without looking at her. She kept helping Betsy make stroking motions as Chuck gently held Rikki in place with a hug.

Chuck's head was close to the dog's, and Betsy's hand suddenly moved from Rikki's face to his. He stayed still, allowing the woman to study him through touch as a blind person might.

She moved back to Rikki, and after about ten minutes, Sheree whispered they should leave before Betsy became too stimulated. Just outside the door, Chuck introduced his dog to Betsy's husband, Jim. Chuck told him about Betsy guessing Rikki was a golden retriever just by touch, and

Jim said they'd had a golden retriever for many years and were also associated with K9s for Warriors. His brother and sister-in-law, Bob and Shari Duval, had started the foundation, which is supported by the Wounded Warrior Project. They adopt and train companion dogs—mostly goldens—to help soldiers suffering from post-traumatic stress disorder and traumatic brain injuries. Soldiers are brought to the K9s for Warriors center and stay for a few weeks while getting to know the dogs. At the end of the visit, the soldiers and dogs choose each other.

It had become a family project; Jim and Betsy's nephew, professional golfer David Duval, had arranged for the PGA Tour to support it as well.

Another uncanny encounter, Chuck thought. How fascinating that a family focused on helping dogs help people—especially with conditions similar to what Betsy was experiencing—was now on the receiving end of that same therapy.

* * *

Four days after Christmas, Rikki was back at work. Her tail and head were high as she led Chuck into the Tallahassee Memorial Rehabilitation Center. It was as if she knew this was where she was supposed to be; she knew what to expect and what to do, and she knew people would be waiting for her.

As he entered Betsy's room, Chuck was faced again with the challenge of how to get Rikki close to Betsy. Because of Betsy's seizures, he dared not let Rikki get up onto the bed, like he'd done with other patients. He lured her over to the mattress again, and Betsy seemed to understand there was a dog in the room but didn't seem quite as aware as she had been on the first visit. She lay curled into a fetal position facing them, then abruptly turned away, then back again.

In the filtered light, Chuck noticed what seemed like hundreds of cards and letters on the walls from family, friends, and organizations. There were photos, too, and looking closer, he recognized the preaccident Betsy: a beautiful red-haired woman with a healthy glow receiving some community service award. Chuck imagined a full life for her, and he hoped Rikki would be able to help her regain that life, but he wondered if that was realistic, considering what the therapists had told him.

The session was short, so Chuck decided to see if Rikki could help Jim Duval, who was sitting on a couch in the hallway talking on his cell phone. Jim reached out for Rikki as they approached and told his caller, "I'm petting the dog I told you about—can I call you back?"

He started stroking Rikki, looking into her face, but quickly pulled away when his emotions began surfacing. Chuck assured him he would come see Betsy on their next trip a week later. Unable to think beyond that day, Jim grimly nodded and said, "Thank you." As they stepped onto the elevator, Chuck decided that even if Rikki couldn't help Betsy next week, they would keep trying to help Jim.

The following Thursday, when Chuck and Rikki arrived at Betsy's door, he heard awful wailing and confused shouting from the room. Sheree entered with them, and they saw two therapists and Jim trying to get Betsy into a reclining chair, but it was a real wrestling match. Betsy was yelling in confusion—not pain—and her body kept balling up and flopping around. She had virtually no motor control, and her eyes remained shut.

Once Betsy was in the chair, Chuck moved Rikki closer, and the dog placed her muzzle on Betsy's arm. But Betsy's body flipped over suddenly, and she kicked Rikki in the back. It wasn't hard enough to hurt, but it was enough to startle the dog and make her wary of that flopping leg. Still, Rikki followed Chuck's lure, putting her head back in position. The team of therapists, Jim Duval, and Chuck were all working to direct Betsy's arms and hands toward the dog's body when she suddenly shouted, "Rikki!" That told Chuck that Betsy and his golden were somehow connecting. After about fifteen minutes, Betsy had relaxed and was no longer yelling. She let Rikki rub against her and was able to run her hand along the dog's head a few times.

One of Betsy's therapists asked Chuck if they could come more frequently, so they returned the next day. As Chuck was getting Rikki out of the car, he saw an ambulance parked in the front. It was not unusual, as emergency medical services (EMS) often transported patients from the acute care unit to rehab and vice versa. As they approached with an empty stretcher, one of the EMS workers shouted, "Rikki!" Chuck was pretty sure they'd never met, but the woman walked over and started rubbing Rikki's head and ears. "So this must be the Rikki we've heard so much about," she said, mostly to the dog. The two other EMS workers petted her briefly as well, and all three were smiling as they walked away. One called back to Rikki, "Go do a good job for those patients!"

Chuck knocked on Betsy's door, knowing her therapists were expecting them. He saw two therapists, including Tracey, with whom they'd worked frequently, supporting Betsy under her arms, moving her to a walker, and then helping her into a reclining chair. Betsy's eyes were tightly closed, and she was moaning. But she occasionally responded to the therapists' commands: "Move your left foot, Betsy" and "You have to use the arms of the chair for support, Betsy—not us."

Once Betsy was awkwardly slumped over in the chair, Tracey told Betsy, "You have a visitor." Tracey asked if Betsy could see the dog. Betsy didn't open her eyes and only moaned a response. Tracey said, "Do you know what Rikki is?" and without hesitation, Betsy replied, "Dog!"

Chuck knelt beside the chair, and Rikki moved toward Betsy's lap. Her legs were nearly straight out, as she was in a half-reclining position, which made it difficult for Rikki to get closer. When Betsy's legs twitched and kicked unexpectedly toward Rikki, the dog moved away, but Chuck coaxed her back. Carrots were working at first, and he managed to get the two close enough so that Rikki's head rubbed against Betsy's arms and hands; a few times, her hand petted Rikki, and everyone could see that it calmed Betsy down.

"Do you have a dog?" Tracey asked.

"Yes," Betsy answered.

"What kind?"

"A golden retriever."

"What's her name?"

Betsy couldn't remember and scowled with frustration. Her torso then fell forward over her lap, and she reached out toward Rikki, as if to examine her more closely.

Chuck noticed Rikki's head moving forward and felt her rear pulling away and realized that Betsy's hand was tugging hard on her leash. He quickly reached out and pried Betsy's fingers off of it, one by one. After disengaging her hand, he repositioned himself and Rikki—leash in one hand, carrots in another, balancing on one knee and trying to avoid getting tangled in tubes. But then Betsy's hand was at it again, this time grabbing the bottom part of Rikki's collar. The golden stayed calm as the woman pulled, but her eyes darted around, an indication that she was stressed. Chuck pried Betsy's hands away again and moved Rikki to a safe distance.

After stroking Rikki's back and flopping her ears the way she liked, he coaxed her back over to Betsy. Rikki was timid but moved closer anyway. The dog gingerly put her nose up to where Betsy could reach it, and Chuck could see she knew Betsy wanted and needed her, but she wasn't sure how to deliver. She finally got her head close enough for Betsy to pet her and touch her ears again, which seemed to calm and quiet the woman.

The following Monday, Chuck heard Betsy yelling and shouting unconnected words from down the hall, but they didn't sound as loud or anxious as before. A therapist asked Chuck if he had any ideas to improve Betsy and Rikki's interaction, and they determined that moving Betsy to a wheelchair might provide better access for Rikki.

Chuck said he wasn't sure if Rikki was going to be cautious after having her collar tugged. But after they opened the door, Rikki went straight for Betsy and placed her head on her lap. Betsy was so different this time. Her vocalizations were quieter, and they didn't have the same confused tone, which always seemed so pain filled.

Rikki nuzzled Betsy's paralyzed left arm, and she leaned back and said, "Safe." As the dog came closer, Betsy paused as if savoring the feeling in an attempt to understand it and said, "Soft."

Tracey was holding Betsy's good hand, and Chuck suggested repositioning again so Betsy could pet Rikki with her working arm. The difference in Betsy's demeanor was immediate. Her face relaxed as she stroked Rikki's head and ear. "Soft," she said again. Then, just as sudden, "Faith."

"That's right," Tracey told her. "Keep the faith."

"Can you see Rikki?" Tracey asked. Betsy's eyelid fluttered a bit, trying to open. Then she reached up with her good arm, used her finger to pry open the lid, and looked at Rikki.

"She likes carrots," Tracey said.

Betsy repeated, "Carrots!"

Chuck said, "Would you like to give Rikki a carrot?" and she answered yes. He put one in her hand and positioned it in a way that Rikki could take it.

The next day, after some quick visits with other patients, Chuck and Rikki arrived at Betsy's door at the appointed time, nine thirty a.m. They had committed to visit every day if possible, as the therapists said consistency was crucial. Jim Duval was outside the room, and he bent down to pet Rikki as they listened to Betsy's wails and shouts from inside the room.

Betsy was in a recliner, so Chuck asked if they could move the chair away from the wall and machines and swivel it 180 degrees to allow Rikki to access Betsy's lap and good arm. This would also give Chuck plenty of room to move around and still protect Rikki.

As soon as the changes were made, Rikki moved close to Betsy without prompting. The woman relaxed as Rikki's head rested on her arm. "No, no, no," she said, although Chuck didn't think she meant it.

The therapists had asked Chuck to bring a brush to add to the interaction, and Beverly, the therapist assigned to Betsy that day, asked her if she would like to brush Rikki. She said yes, so Beverly placed the brush in Betsy's right hand and directed the motion. Tears streamed down Betsy's face, and she was quiet while stroking the dog.

* * *

Two days later, after an extended twenty-five-minute session with Betsy, Chuck and Rikki ran into Sheree in the hallway. Tracey joined them and was talking about Betsy's latest AAT session—a really good one. Sheree seemed a bit distracted, but Chuck didn't think anything of it until he noticed Rikki staring straight up at her. Rikki leaned against Sheree's leg, and she crouched down to pet her. Chuck said, "She's really keying in on you, Sheree. Is everything okay?"

Not really, she admitted. The nineteen-year-old daughter of her close friend was admitted to the hospital the night before and was in a coma. She was diagnosed with spinal meningitis—often fatal—and Sheree had spent most of the night with the girl and her family. They didn't know if she was going to live. All morning, Sheree had worn her "public face," and up until that moment, no one had seen through it. But Rikki had.

After stroking Rikki, Sheree looked up at Chuck. "How did she know?" It was a question that he and other pet therapy team members heard frequently but never quite knew how to answer.

Rikki snoozed on the backseat on their twenty-minute ride home, but when she stepped out of the SUV, she took the leash into her mouth and became playful. She looked back at Chuck with a sly grin and shook the leash, then pranced up to the front steps and waited for him to open the door. Inside, she gave a brief growl toward Milo, the neighbor's dog who had adopted the Mitchells, then headed for her sister Loosey, another rescue they'd recently acquired. The two girls barked excitedly, so Chuck let them out to burn off energy. After about fifteen minutes of play, Rikki was back at the door, ready for a long nap on the couch.

On one of their regular rounds at the rehab center, Chuck saw Sheree and Jim Duval talking in the hallway, and she was still marveling about how Rikki had picked up on her distress and zeroed in on her. Usually, the dog lay down and took a break when they stood in the hall and chatted, but not that time. Sheree said Rikki was staring at her with those knowing eyes. Jim smiled and nodded his head; he knew that feeling.

Sheree admitted that when the animal therapy teams first came through the rehab facility, she thought, *Oh, these are just dog people,* as if dogs were just filling a void in their owners' lives. But after a few encounters with

Rikki, she said she changed her view. She now believed there were people and animals called to this volunteer service the same way the medical staffers were to their professions—it was a true gift.

On the next visit, they saw Jim Duval working on his iPad in the alcove. Rikki made a beeline for him, and he reached out, smiling. Chuck had not seen Betsy in a while and wondered how she was doing. That day had not been the best, but overall she had made a lot of progress. Betsy was walking the hallways regularly and even asked Jim about the car accident that led to her injuries. He conceded that it was still a stop-and-start process. Betsy was getting a bath, so Chuck said he and Rikki would see other patients and check back later.

When they walked into Betsy's room later in the morning, she was in a recliner. That didn't stop Rikki from going toward her outstretched arm. Chuck had a carrot lure ready to get Rikki closer, but he didn't have to use it. He noticed Betsy's eyelids were open wider. She began stroking Rikki with her right hand. Rikki looked right up at her face, and Betsy said, "What a beautiful dog," then leaned forward and reached for her, like the time she had grabbed Rikki's leash. But Chuck didn't think it would happen this time. Rikki was relaxed and didn't look like she sensed any danger, either.

Betsy thanked them—twice—before they left. Closing the door behind them, Chuck knew he had just gotten a glimpse of the preaccident Betsy. She was coming back.

* * *

Because of conflicts in their schedule and Betsy's, it was another three weeks before Chuck and Rikki spent time with her again. Chuck was getting reports from Sheree that her progress had accelerated, and she was optimistic Betsy was going to make a full recovery—or at least something close to it. All of the therapists were calling it a miracle.

Chuck had shadowed his wife, Patty, on her READ visits in the schools the previous day, so Patty was accompanying him and Rikki to rehab. Several therapists told Chuck that Betsy's cognition had improved but that she didn't remember much about the therapy sessions, including those with Rikki.

When they entered the room, Betsy was sitting in a big chair, dressed in street clothes. She didn't have any braces, arm splints, or tubes hanging from her body. Her husband, Jim, was across from her. When Sheree told Betsy she had a visitor, Rikki went straight for her lap.

"Oh, what a beautiful dog!" she said. Sheree explained that they were a pet therapy team and had been visiting her the last few months. Betsy's hands stayed on Rikki, and the dog remained close, even as the woman leaned over her.

Jim told his wife how often Chuck and Rikki had come and asked if she remembered the dog's name. She did not, but she remembered touching her. She apologized to Chuck since she didn't remember him, either, but he said,

"Hey, it's nice to meet you, Betsy." It felt like it really was his first time meeting her—the real Betsy.

Sheree left, and Chuck and Patty remained behind with Rikki. Jim and Betsy talked about the lambs, turkeys, possums, and raccoons they had rescued and kept as pets over the years. Chuck and Patty were surprised to hear that the couple had lived off a road near theirs early in the Mitchells' marriage. Who knows, they might have even crossed paths back then and never known it.

Betsy became emotional at times but had begun to make light of her circumstances. She said she asked Jim to make up a sign for her to wear that said, "I'm sorry if I don't remember you, but it's okay—give me a little time."

A week later, Chuck received an e-mail from Sheree saying Betsy was going to be discharged from their rehab center in a few days. She was being moved to another center in Sarasota to transition, which would be followed by six weeks of outpatient therapy.

* * *

Nearly a year after the accident, the woman who was so broken up that her doctors thought she'd never recover was talking on the phone excitedly—mostly about Rikki.

She was trying to explain what she called the "coming back."

"The first thing that makes you realize that you're still alive and able to feel is a feeling in your hands . . . it's

not something your brain does." With the electronic cir-
cuitry all confused, Rikki's touch was like a lightning rod,
grounding Betsy's thoughts. She said Rikki helped bring
her spirit up and out of the confused world she was inhab-
iting, reaching into the very depths of her soul.

Rikki "opened up the door that needed opening."

She tried to explain it more in a letter to Tallahassee
Memorial Rehabilitation Center:

> *I call it "Coming Back." If you haven't been there
> (I hope you never are), there is no way for you to
> know what it feels like to become aware of the fact
> that you are alive. For me to be able to think this
> and write it down is a blessing that has taken me
> over a year and a half to be able to do. Just emerg-
> ing from a coma, learning to breathe right, swal-
> low, chew again, see, speak, move my eyes, move
> a finger, hear and understand what someone says,
> is like emerging as a newborn baby. Being able to
> realize that somehow this has happened to you
> before and you are emerging again.*

Betsy credited Rikki with being a vital member of her
care team:

> *Another part of my 'coming back' moments was a
> soft, moist nuzzle in the palm of my hand. Chuck
> Mitchell had brought Rikki . . . to my bedside and*

[she] was putting [her] nose in the palm of my hand. We don't emotionally relate the same way to people as we do to animals. They don't judge you, and you instinctively know that. It's easier to give those feelings out to an animal. For me, the dog is the one I feel in my soul. It touches the soft spot. It is like what gives you a tiny light that you follow 'til it becomes brighter and brighter and your mind opens up wider as you come into it.

CHAPTER 12

COURTROOM CANINE

In January 2013, as Chuck and Rikki closed in on their three hundredth visit, Chuck received a call for a "meet and greet" at the courthouse with a ten-year-old girl and her mother. The mom would be testifying at a hearing the following day, and she and her daughter would both be testifying in a trial later that month. They had reviewed the therapy animal profile book and chosen Rikki.

Susan Parmalee met Chuck and Rikki in the court-house lobby and walked with them to the state attorney's office to meet the victim and her mother. A lithe brown-skinned child jumped up from her seat and shouted, "Rikki!" An attractive woman in her midforties trailed her, and Susan introduced LaRee and Ms. Freeman to Rikki.

Susan rarely introduced Chuck to anyone. Whether it was by design or not, Chuck felt it was somehow appropriate. Rikki was the one they needed to remember.

Rikki moved quietly toward LaRee in greeting, then stayed close to her as they walked through the halls and took the elevator to Susan's office. Kathy Ray, the assistant state attorney prosecuting the case, joined them. She owned two dogs—a golden retriever and a fluffy white Samoyed. Though Susan's office was cramped for five chairs and a dog, Rikki, with her trademark "smile," was 100 percent focused on LaRee. Rikki settled in, lying down with her front paws touching LaRee's feet and her rear paws on Ms. Freeman.

Rikki's strategic positioning caught Kathy and Susan's attention, and the conversation turned toward this remarkable therapy dog. LaRee and Ms. Freeman began petting Rikki, and LaRee gave her a bear hug. Chuck told them about Rikki being a "Katrina baby," and Ms. Freeman said the same hurricane had displaced her family from their home in Baton Rouge. That was where LaRee's father had first victimized his daughter, when she was only four.

Susan and Kathy's plan was to have LaRee watch the hour-long video of the girl's forensics interview to help her give clear and accurate testimony at the trial. They wanted her mother to be out of the room, since she was a witness, but LaRee became anxious about seeing the video without her. Susan directed her attention back to Rikki, and as LaRee relaxed, she set up the video. Her mother said she had to go put money in the parking meter and would be right back.

Susan moved to one side of LaRee, and Chuck to the other with Rikki in front of and under her chair. During the first part of the video, LaRee dropped her head, and her lip quivered with emotion. Rikki moved closer, and LaRee started brushing the dog and feeding her carrots from the Ziploc Chuck had given her. When the video-taped interview covered specifics of the abuse, LaRee reached down and wrapped her arms around Rikki in a long hug, and the dog relaxed into her embrace.

About fifteen minutes into the recording, LaRee's attention was fading. Susan suggested she get on the floor with Rikki to make it easier to pet and hug the dog. LaRee lowered herself and began slowly and gently brushing the dog's golden locks. As much as Chuck tried not to listen to the story, he pieced together enough to know that this child had suffered four years of brutality at the hands of her father, until she had finally confided in a cousin. He looked at LaRee and thought she seemed like a strong yet gentle girl. He knew she was about to endure the ultimate test of both traits.

The interviewer in the video was using drawings to clarify specific body parts. LaRee hugged Rikki as she listened and then lay down on the floor and draped an arm across Rikki's chest.

When the video stopped, Ms. Freeman came into the room and said it was time for them to leave. LaRee kissed Rikki's head several times as they said good-bye, and Susan gave the child a stuffed "Rikki doll" to take with her. Chuck said Rikki would see them the next day.

After helping Rikki into the backseat of his SUV, Chuck climbed into the driver's seat and gripped the steering wheel. He felt a mix of sadness for the girl's trauma and gratitude for Rikki being a channel to help her and her mother get through the ordeal. He wiped his eyes and looked in the rearview mirror. His gifted golden was fast asleep.

The next morning, Susan briefed Chuck on their way upstairs. Their assignment for the day was to keep LaRee occupied while her mother was questioned during a hearing. Her ex-husband—LaRee's father and the defendant— would be present. As difficult as Chuck knew it would be for LaRee's mother, he hoped to use the time to get to know the girl better and not see her through the lens of what he had learned through the video.

In the kids' area of the victim advocate office, there wasn't much room for Rikki to relax, so Susan suggested they go outside. LaRee helped hold the leash as they walked down the hallway and out onto the street. The sun had come out, and LaRee sprinted ahead, then came back to circle around Rikki. The dog responded playfully, mouthing her leash as if she had control of it. Chuck was concerned about Rikki getting overstimulated, but as they walked back through the entrance of the courthouse, she returned to being a calm and quiet therapy dog.

The group went up to the third floor and sat outside of the courtrooms on a row of benches at the end of a long hallway. LaRee stroked Rikki with a doll comb they had found in the kids' play area, since Chuck had forgotten to pack her brush. When the girl asked if she could braid Rikki's hair, Chuck said of course, if she could find enough of it. LaRee examined Rikki all over and finally started twisting and braiding the feathery strands on her side and her legs. There wasn't enough hair to hold the braid, but LaRee smiled contentedly as she tried.

When Ms. Freeman came out of the courtroom and joined them, LaRee demonstrated the tricks she had learned with her new friend. She showed how Rikki would take carrots in a "kiss," and Ms. Freeman's face began to relax.

She told LaRee they had a long drive ahead and needed to say their good-byes. Chuck promised he would see them again when they came back to town for the trial.

Susan called Chuck about three weeks later, on a Friday afternoon. She asked if he and Rikki could meet LaRee and her mother on the coming Sunday and Monday afternoons in preparation for the trial Tuesday morning. He said he would clear his schedule.

Downtown Tallahassee was quiet when Chuck and Rikki arrived on Sunday afternoon, and only a few people—plus one dog—passed by them as they waited outside the entrance of the courthouse. Rikki was relaxed and paid attention only to Chuck until she zeroed in on the ten-year-old coming up the sidewalk, still nearly a block away. Rikki's tail swayed in recognition as she waited patiently for Chuck to take her to LaRee.

Mother and daughter had just driven four hours from their Central Florida home. They visited with Rikki and Chuck under the breezeway until Susan arrived and led them into the empty courthouse. Rikki was focused completely on the little girl, and Chuck felt relieved—no carrots needed on this visit. He had brought two brushes with him, and he told LaRee he had purposely not brushed Rikki so she could do it.

Rikki stayed by the girl's side through the halls and on the elevator. In Susan's office, Rikki rubbed against Ms. Freeman and LaRee until both of them were occupied with petting the dog. Susan reached out as well, and Chuck recalled that the victim advocate rarely did that when they had first begun working together. She had realized that petting the dog was a good thing for everyone.

When Kathy, the prosecutor, arrived they talked about the court procedures. She said the judge would still have to rule on their request to have a dog in the courtroom for the trial, but she was trying to remain optimistic. The title of being the first therapy dog to legally enter a Florida courtroom during trial had gone to a miniature dachshund named Honey Girl the previous fall. Rikki was on vacation with Chuck and Patty at the time, recovering from a brief cancer scare and surgery.

Kathy paused and looked at LaRee, who was smiling and petting Rikki. Kathy asked LaRee if she knew there was going to be a trial on Tuesday and if she thought she was ready to talk about what had happened between her and her father. LaRee's face dropped, and she looked down. She covered her ears with her hands.

Susan moved closer. She told LaRee she had done nothing wrong—that her father was the guilty one. Everyone was proud of her, and what she was doing would protect other girls from having to endure what she'd gone through. LaRee took her hands away from her ears, slowly brushed Rikki, then fingered her silky ears.

Someone asked LaRee if she was scared. She said, "A little bit."

Susan asked, "What about it scares you, LaRee?"

She shrugged. "That there will be people there." LaRee said she didn't care about what would happen to her father, but she just didn't want to talk about it in front of strangers.

"Can you tell us just a little bit about what happened?" Kathy asked.

Again, silence. After a few minutes, Kathy suggested they go outside to walk Rikki and enjoy the weather. Chuck fished a second leash out of his pack, hooked it on the dog's collar, and gave the other end to LaRee to hold. From experience, he knew that not every child could handle the second leash without jerking it, but he felt that with the way LaRee moved, she would be fine.

On the green space outside, LaRee collected flowers, acorns, and twigs to present one at a time to Rikki. She asked the dog which she liked best. Rikki nosed each item LaRee presented and even mouthed some of them.

When LaRee moved to the far edge of the sidewalk, out of earshot, Chuck asked Susan how she felt about the trial. "I am worried," she answered plainly. "I don't know if LaRee will be able to testify in front of her father."

Hearing that stark possibility, Chuck's heart sank. He thought back on his previous interactions with LaRee and realized that Susan was right. This was their third visit with LaRee, and he had yet to hear her speak one word about the abuse. Yes, there had been the hour-long video where she painstakingly gave details, but Chuck had never heard LaRee say anything about it in person.

The tape was very compelling, Susan said, and it would be played first—out of the presence of the mother and child—but the girl would need to verify and corroborate enough of the facts to convince the jury.

Chuck realized that all he and Rikki could do was give their best and hope that LaRee would find the strength to testify when things got tough.

For pretrial prep the next day, Chuck and Rikki met the group in the courthouse atrium, and Rikki went straight to LaRee. The girl knelt down and wrapped her arms around the dog in a familiar hug. A man named Sam came into Susan's office and introduced himself to LaRee. He said he would see her the next day. Later, Chuck learned that Sam was the defense attorney and was there on two missions: to build rapport with LaRee and to check out this therapy dog that might be the child's "comfort item" in court.

When Sam left, Kathy sat on the floor next to LaRee, and Rikki moved over to be within petting distance of both of them. Kathy asked if LaRee would like to talk about what had happened with her father, but the girl just got quiet and focused more intently on brushing Rikki and doing her "kiss" trick with the carrot.

Kathy suggested they see the courtroom where they would be the next day, and LaRee smiled—she'd never been inside a courtroom. Chuck was just as interested, as he needed to survey the surroundings and work out the best strategy for following the courtroom protocols.

The floor was carpeted, and the benches in the gallery area were like wooden church pews. The backs were high enough to hide Rikki from the view of the jury—as the protocol required that the jurors not be aware a dog was in the courtroom, an effort to avoid distracting or influencing them in any way. Chuck also removed Rikki's tags to prevent them from jingling.

Kathy walked LaRee through a few simple questions, but Susan noticed that the girl kept looking at her mother, seated in the gallery, before responding. Susan whispered to Ms. Freeman, and they walked into the hallway together while Kathy continued asking questions. Chuck could see that LaRee was shutting down, so he held a carrot up just high enough over the back of the bench in front of them, and Rikki poked her nose over the top to get it. The move caught the girl's attention. Kathy moved closer to the witness stand, and LaRee looked down for a moment. Quietly, she began describing the various places, times, and ways that her father had raped her.

Chuck was relieved when a female bailiff came to sit on the bench next to him and stroked Rikki. She whispered, "Even armed deputies need stress relief." Chuck marveled at how much affection the deputy had for Rikki. Then she told him she'd lost all her dogs the previous year—right after her father had died.

Kathy told LaRee she had done well, and they all returned to Susan's office. Ms. Freeman said she and LaRee would try to see a movie that night, but they would be back around eight the next morning for the eight thirty trial. The rest of the group stayed to talk over procedural questions, since it was the first trial in which Chuck and Kathy would be working together with a dog in the courtroom.

Before Chuck and Rikki left for the day, Kathy turned to him and said, "You know, if it wasn't for Rikki, I don't think we would be able to prosecute this case. LaRee wouldn't be able to do it without Rikki, and we can't do it without her testimony."

Susan and Kathy both hugged Rikki good-bye, and as good as the day had been, Chuck knew he would be sleeping anxiously that night.

The next day brought summerlike weather, even though it was midwinter. Chuck left extra early in case he hit traffic and arrived forty-five minutes before the scheduled meeting time. He and Rikki walked around the green space, then visited with the deputies working security before they headed upstairs.

When they arrived, it was clear that LaRee's mother had followed LaRee's therapist's advice of making the day seem special. For a ten-year-old girl, that meant a fashion statement. Her hair was braided tight across her head and gathered in an updo, grown-up style. Her colorfully striped T-shirt was topped with a cropped faded-denim jacket, and straight-leg jeans just grazed the top of her blue canvas sneakers. LaRee's toothy smile made it clear she felt just as cute inside.

Walking through the hallways, Rikki remained close to LaRee. Chuck had hooked up the second leash, and the dog and girl kept the same pace, as if they'd been together for years.

On the benches immediately outside the courtroom, LaRee's increased anxiety expressed itself in her nonstop talking. Her therapist had given her "worry rocks," miniature marbles that could serve as a comfort item. When Rikki reclined, the girl tried balancing them on the dog's ribs. LaRee then began braiding Rikki's tail—something most dogs would not tolerate, but the golden lay perfectly still.

Chuck sat on the floor on one side of Rikki as LaRee worked the other side. He wanted to make sure his dog didn't show signs of stress. But Rikki's relaxed mouth, closed eyes, and steady breathing assured him all was well in Rikki's world.

Kathy came over and told Chuck that he and Rikki could come into the courtroom for pretrial motions and witness instructions. The jury would not be present. Chuck's stomach tightened as he remembered someone saying that Judge James Hankinson was a stickler about courtroom procedures and was still among the skeptics regarding dogs in the courtroom. He knew that Rikki would be moved in and out of court when the jury was on break—as would LaRee—and that the judge would have to consider a mistrial if there was any problem, such as the dog causing a distraction.

As Chuck and Rikki sat in the gallery, Judge Hankinson turned to Kathy, the prosecutor, and referenced the therapy dog. "There is a little bit of a risk involved—are you willing to take that risk?"

"Yes, your honor," she said. Chuck swallowed hard.

The judge granted the motion to have a therapy dog present, as long as it was according to protocols. He had no objection to the worry stones, either.

Back on the corridor benches, as they waited for the girl and her mother to be called, LaRee continued to occupy herself with Rikki. "Okay, are you ready?" she asked the dog. "Shake." Rikki offered a right paw. "Good girl."

She told Rikki ghost stories and gave her a spelling lesson: "Five is spelled f-i-v-e." Then she worked it into a math lesson: "You have five toes. Five times two is ten."

In a relaxed pose, paws crossed in front of her, Rikki looked at LaRee and then back at Chuck for a check-in.

Ms. Freeman was called into the courtroom first, and when she came out thirty minutes later, she rushed by her daughter and went straight to the ladies' room. Chuck could see that LaRee wanted to follow, so he distracted her with a carrot. "Why don't you give Rikki a treat?"

This led to more tricks, as LaRee balanced a worry stone on her own nose while spreading her arms out and said, "Rikki, look at this." Then she tried to repeat the trick on Rikki's nose when she was lying down. She studied the dog from head to tail and told Chuck she most admired her long eyelashes.

Chuck told LaRee about Rikki's boyfriend, the Great Dane Grendel, and how Grendel had horses at his house. He directed her to Rikki's favorite spots for stroking (ears and tummy) and complimented her. "You're nice and gentle with Rikki—that's why she's loving you so much, because you're gentle."

As the time dragged on, LaRee lay on her back and used Rikki's body as a pillow.

Ms. Freeman joined them again, and she asked Rikki's age. Seven and a half, Chuck said, then he told her about the cancer surgery she'd had the previous year. The vet was very optimistic; Rikki was a survivor.

Kathy came out of the courtroom and asked LaRee, "Are you ready?" The girl was in the middle of telling Rikki a story about a pirate, so Kathy let her finish.

LaRee stood up, and Kathy whispered something in her ear as they entered the courtroom, Chuck and Rikki trailing behind. LaRee gave Kathy a squeeze around the waist before they walked into court. Chuck and Rikki sat in the back left corner of the gallery area, out of sight of the jury box, and LaRee walked slowly across the courtroom and up to the witness chair. As Kathy pulled away from LaRee, the girl grabbed her around her neck and held tight. The attorney whispered some consoling words, and the girl dropped her arms. LaRee turned around to face the courtroom—with her dad, the accused, in front—and bowed her head. She then put one hand on her forehead and balled the other in a fist in front of her face.

The bailiff knocked twice. "All rise." LaRee stood. Judge Hankinson entered, and after he took his seat, the bailiff knocked again and all rose as the jury entered.

LaRee sat down and bowed her head again, fists on her forehead, hiding her eyes. When Kathy started asking her questions, LaRee spoke clearly, giving her name and spelling it. She then gave her father's name and answered that she used to live in Tallahassee with her mother, brother, sister, and dad. She said yes, there were times that her dad would take care of her when her mother was at work.

"During those times, did he ever touch your body in a way that you didn't like—such as your private parts?"

LaRee's voice quieted and her hands moved to completely cover her face and eyes. "Yes, ma'am."

"Tell us what he would do when that would happen."

Silence. Chuck's stomach tensed; she was freezing up again. But he didn't dare try to lure Rikki's nose over the bench like before, at the risk of giving grounds for a mistrial. Maybe Susan was right—and LaRee wouldn't be able to do this.

Another minute went by, which felt like forever in the somber courtroom.

LaRee then whispered, "He would . . ." A female jury member leaned forward, and a few others shifted in their chairs. "He would put his private part in my mouth and in my bottom."

Kathy thanked her and told the judge those were all her questions. The defense attorney's follow-up was brief—he wanted to know where LaRee went to school and whether she had been in after-school care.

The judge excused the jury, and when they were gone, Kathy led LaRee to the swinging doors, where Susan was waiting. Chuck and Rikki trailed the two to the benches outside. LaRee ran to her mother, wrapped her arms around her waist, and buried her face in her side; Susan rested a hand on LaRee's opposite shoulder. Kathy came out and told LaRee how well she'd done. She bowed her head shyly and received Kathy's hug.

Ms. Freeman moved her daughter to a bench, and Rikki sat in front of LaRee and looked up at her face. LaRee wrapped both arms around the dog's neck and leaned close between Chuck and Rikki. "Thank you so much for being here for me," she whispered. "I couldn't have done it without you." She turned to look into the dog's eyes and added, "I will never forget you, Rikki."

Chuck's throat tightened. "Thank you, LaRee . . . That's just why Rikki's here." He turned away slightly and wiped his eyes, hoping she didn't notice.

In the quiet that followed, Chuck pondered the moment more. Though his dog could not talk, she had helped this little girl—this victim of horrible abuse—find her voice when it was needed most.

LaRee's anxiety lessened, and Rikki also relaxed, eventually lying down. LaRee began brushing and braiding again, and her bubbly side resurfaced.

Kathy expressed concern that the jurors might be coming through the hallways, so they moved to Susan's office to wait for the verdict. Ms. Freeman told Chuck she had never really been a dog person, but Rikki had made her rethink her feelings about dogs and what they could do for people.

No longer needed in an official capacity, Chuck said it was time for him and Rikki to say good-bye. LaRee squeezed Rikki's neck tight, and both LaRee and her mom said they would never forget Rikki.

Chuck looked at his watch—a little past noon. He and Rikki had been at it for five intense hours, and he was emotionally drained. Yet he was so relieved that LaRee had been able to testify and that Rikki had been so perfect in the courtroom. They were approaching the third anniversary of that pivotal trial when Zoe had hugged Rikki outside of the courtroom and begged Chuck for her to come inside.

Still, he thought, his success with Rikki would be hollow if LaRee's abuser walked. Later that afternoon, Chuck answered a call from Susan. She and Kathy were on speakerphone to announce the news: LaRee's father was found guilty on all counts. Chuck jumped up and pumped his fists in exultation. He was happy for LaRee and her mom—and Rikki.

As with Frank Dieter's case, Chuck knew the verdict carried a mandatory life sentence with no parole. There would be no chance for him to victimize other children in his lifetime.

Susan had other news for Chuck—this case had a distinction in the courthouse therapy dog program. While this was the Second Judicial Circuit's third trial with a therapy team, this was the first that actually resulted in a conviction. LaRee's father's case couldn't be appealed, either, so Rikki had earned yet another permanent place in the record books.

Chuck realized that what Zoe and Rikki had inspired had come true. Because of them, LaRee and other children would not have to walk into the courtroom alone when facing their abuser. He felt privileged to be teamed up with the dog that had inspired the law that had changed everything.

EPILOGUE

By 2015, the ten-year anniversary of Hurricane Katrina, Chuck and Rikki had logged more than five hundred visits as a therapy dog team, and Rikki had made nearly three hundred visits with Patty through the READ program. Rikki was also celebrating her tenth birthday. To mark that milestone, Chuck and Patty were planning to take the dog on a weeklong vacation at pet-friendly beach destinations around Florida.

Much like she's lived her life, the little golden has aged gracefully. Veterinarian Julia Stege is monitoring her hip dysplasia, common to Rikki's breed, and removed another cancerous lump, but she is optimistic for the dog's full recovery.

In March, Rikki's big brother, Roscoe, suffered a ruptured spleen and died suddenly. He was approaching his eleventh birthday. Rikki's Great Dane "boyfriend," Grendel, retired from active pet therapy visits the following month at age ten.

Rikki has continued to work, but not at the same levels as in the past, even though she never shows signs of her own discomfort while comforting others.

About once a year, Chuck and Rikki enjoy a special visit with Zoe and her family when they travel to Tallahassee to see their relatives. Zoe's mother, Danielle, captures the moments in photos, which resemble a family reunion. In one particular image, the dark-haired thirteen-year-old sits cross-legged on a patch of grass at a park, hugging Rikki. Zoe's eyes are softly closed and her face expresses peace, thanksgiving—the way someone would relate to a rescuer. *You got me through it all.*

Chuck records details about these and other visits in a journal that he's kept from the beginning. It helps him keep track of and mentally process the encounters, including some of the ones he found extraordinary. He described one visit when he and Rikki were introduced to a man named Warren who was recovering from his sixth hip-replacement surgery. As Warren stroked Rikki, Chuck told him about her being a Katrina rescue. The gentleman volunteered that he had taken care of two golden retriever puppies that had also been rescued from Hurricane Katrina. He said it was while he was serving on the board of directors of the Humane Society. They had asked him and his wife to help out as a favor, and he had always wondered what had happened to those puppies.

Warren's story had a familiar ring. Chuck stared at him, as Warren continued to stroke Rikki. Could it be? He peered at Rikki, and she had that knowing look, as if Warren was not a stranger. Chuck asked a few more questions and finally said, "Well, you're not going to believe this. But you're looking at one of the puppies you helped rescue."

Warren looked down at Rikki and back at Chuck, and laughed as if he couldn't believe his good fortune. Rikki placed her paw on his leg, and Chuck better explained the story about how he and Patty came to be Rikki's new pet parents. Warren moved his hand across the top of her head and studied her further. Finally, he met the dog's eyes and smiled. "You've come a long way, baby."

Years after this encounter, when Chuck was serving as an evaluator for animal therapy teams, Warren showed up at the center to be screened with his latest rescue, a golden retriever named Chance. After breezing through the evaluation among the top of the twenty-two teams screened that evening, Warren expressed hope of one day shadowing Chuck and Rikki at the rehab center.

In another uncanny encounter, on April 1, 2014, Chuck, Patty, and Rikki were standing outside of the twenty-two-story Florida Capitol in downtown Tallahassee. They were there to witness legislation being signed into law to broaden the use of therapy dogs in the courts, such as in cases involving intellectually disabled and other vulnerable witnesses. A small group of people stopped to pet Rikki, and Chuck was telling them a little about her when a woman came up beside him. "You're Chuck Mitchell, aren't you?"

He turned around. "Yes, and this is my therapy dog, Rikki." The woman knelt down next to Rikki and stroked her head. "Of course, I'd recognize *her*. I have Rikki's sister!"

Melinda Piller explained that when Hurricane Katrina hit, she was a consultant for the Humane Society. When she heard the office staffers talking about a mother dog and her two puppies being surrendered, she mentioned it to her husband, who was undergoing treatment for prostate cancer. "He had never asked anything for himself his whole life," she told Chuck and Patty, but he wanted one of those puppies.

Melinda admitted that she was hesitant, as they already had a Great Dane and she was helping to care for her elderly mother. But she put a request in, paid a fee, and after passing the home inspection, they received the dog. The Humane Society volunteers had named her "Diana," but her husband renamed her "Girlie."

The golden brought a lot of joy to their home, especially during the end stages of her husband's disease. "We call her the angel dog," Melinda said. "She tolerated everything."

Melinda remembered being told that Girlie had a sister with the Mitchells, and she recognized Chuck from his former construction business. She had always intended to connect, but it just had never happened, until she saw them at the capitol.

Chuck marveled at the encounter, and he and Patty told Melinda a little more about Rikki. They determined there were some distinct differences. Girlie is larger than Rikki and has a thicker coat. Unlike Rikki, she also gets along famously with other canines. Melinda told them, "Girlie hasn't ever met a dog she doesn't love."

Perhaps the most mysterious encounter took place in December 2014, while Chuck and Rikki were visiting the Florida State Hospital in Chattahoochee. They had not been to this particular specialty care unit in more than a year. When they entered the therapy room, Chuck saw dozens of patients sitting in a circle of chairs, and one man caught his eye. He had long hair and a beard and was shaking uncontrollably, as if he had Parkinson's or another disease that caused tremors. He shook so much that Chuck wasn't even sure he was aware of Rikki, as they visited the gentleman sitting next to him. When they started to move past him, the shaky man reached out to try to pet the golden, but his arm was vibrating so much it didn't seem like they would be able to connect. Rikki stopped, and Chuck noted that she wasn't afraid; she even leaned a bit closer to him. Still, his arm could only bump up and down across her back. Chuck tried to look at the man's eyes, but they were shaking back and forth in their sockets, and he decided it would be better to focus on the arm bumping across Rikki. Suddenly, the bouncing stopped and the man's hand began to gently stroke Rikki's coat in a smooth and normal motion. Chuck looked up at his face and was stunned to see he had a calm demeanor and a gentle, reassuring smile. The man met Chuck's gaze and asked how Rikki's was doing with her cancer.

Chuck's response was automatic, even as he tried to remember if they had ever met before. "She's doing fine."

The man asked, "Did the second surgery go okay, too?"

Still baffled, his mind racing as he tried to figure out where or how the man could have gotten that information, Chuck said, "Yes, it did."

"And the cancer was just under the skin, right?" the man said.

"That's right," Chuck told him. *Where the heck did he get this information?*

"And they call it mast cell?"

Chuck nodded his reply, still searching the man's eyes for something familiar. Acknowledging Chuck's answer, he looked back at Rikki and quietly but firmly said, "She should be just fine."

Just as abruptly, the man's tremors returned, and his eyes began wiggling in their sockets. Chuck had to look away, but as stunned as he felt, he sensed a great wave of warmth and comfort from the encounter. *How did he know that Rikki would be fine?* And what made Chuck *think* that he knew?

Another patient jerked Chuck's attention away by thrusting a drawing he had made of Rikki in front of him, and the visit was over. But Chuck kept pondering the encounter. He later asked some of the therapists if they had any information on the shaky man. No one knew a patient matching that description. In a follow-up correspondence, the volunteer coordinator said, "I think you might very well have experienced an angel, Chuck."

ACKNOWLEDGMENTS

The idea of writing about pet therapy teams came out of a chance encounter at the post office with Chuck Mitchell. I had interviewed him on previous journalism assignments and had always found him fascinating. This book project launched when I asked quite casually, "So, Chuck, what are you doing these days?"

I am tremendously indebted to him and his wife, Patty, who were willing to open up their lives to the deep interrogation required by the craft of literary journalism. They allowed me to tag along, hosted me at their home, and connected me to their world in a way many people would rather avoid. To the two of you and the rest of your pack—Milo, Rikki, Loosey, and CB the cat—big wags. Rikki, you truly are my hero.

This book started as my thesis for the master of fine arts in creative nonfiction program at Goucher College. Thank you to authors Allan Zullo, Ned Stuckey-French, and Heidi Tyline King for recommending me for the program. To my Goucher mentors, Suzannah Lessard, Leslie Rubinkowski, Tom French, Richard Todd, Joanne Wyckoff, and the previous director Patsy Sims, please know that you changed my life. I have a new appreciation for story and have enjoyed using the tools you shared for working on long-form narrative.

Diana Hume George, I didn't get to work closely with you at Goucher, but we sure are making up for it now. Your guidance on this and other writing projects has helped me apply what I learned in that program. I can't say enough about what your wise guidance and encouragement has meant.

I'm grateful to all the individuals involved in pet therapy and dog behavior and training who took the time to educate me, including Stephanie Perkins and her team at the TMH Animal Therapy Program, as well as Stephanie Bell, Jean Hewitt, Shirley Roux, Allie Howell, Jay and Sam King, veterinarian Julia Stege, and vet tech Destiny Martel; to former Leon County Humane Society program director Melissa Abernathy, who helped me rebuild Rikki's story; to Haven Cook and Laura Bevans for educating me on disaster-related rescue; and to those in the courts—Susan Wilson, Helene Potlock, Susan Parmalee, and John Hutchins among them. To Allie Phillips, who is at the forefront of animal behavior and human-animal bond issues, I am so grateful for your wisdom and your work. And to a supremely gifted individual who patiently shared her story about rescuing pets in the aftermath of Hurricane Katrina but declined to be named, you know who you are—I am grateful.

To the many people at Tallahassee Memorial HealthCare, most especially Sheree Porter and the rehabilitation therapists willing to give animal-assisted therapy a try, congratulations and thank you.

To all who helped in my research—Beth Liljestrand, Kim Ellis, staffers at the First District Court of Appeal and the Leon County Sheriff's Office—I owe you! And to Lauren Book of Lauren's Kids, and attorney and lobbyist Ron Book, your contributions to furthering the use of therapy dogs in Florida is beyond measure.

Betsy Duval, please know that you have inspired so many of us with your story of "coming back." Thank you for allowing me a glimpse into that world. To the child victims, whose identities have been veiled, and their parents who allowed me to include their stories, please know that you are all heroes. Because of you, other children will be protected from abuse, and victims can avoid being further traumatized as justice is served.

I'm grateful to fellow pet lover, transcriptionist Genevieve Van de Merghel, who hung in there during this four-year process, and to the creative minds that helped with websites and book trailers: Al and George Cuneo, Gary Yordon, and C. B. Lorch. I'm especially indebted to publisher Larry Levitsky and his capable team at Inkshares for "rescuing" this manuscript, and to those who gave it a vigorous polish and saw it through production, including Clete Barrett Smith and Girl Friday Productions. To all who furthered along the process by supporting the project online, especially Paula Fortunas and the Tallahassee Memorial HealthCare Foundation, thank you.

Jim Bettinger, I saved you for last. Thank you for putting up with all of my writing projects these last thirty-two years—and most of all for your prayers during this new chapter in my life.

ABOUT THE AUTHOR

Julie Strauss Bettinger received her master of fine arts in creative nonfiction from Goucher College in 2013. Her work as a freelance writer spans twenty-five years, primarily for publications in Florida and the southeast United States. Her writing appears in *Florida Trend*, *Florida Small Business*, FSU's *Research in Review*, and *Florida State Law* magazine. She wrote a weekly business column for the *Tallahassee Democrat* and was the editor of *Tallahassee* and *Emerald Coast* magazines. For nearly twenty years she was the editor for two law-enforcement journals. Her published works include the coauthored book *Blasted by Adversity: The Making of a Wounded Warrior*, published by Inkshares in May 2015.

For more information, visit www.JulieBettinger.com.

LIST OF PATRONS

This book was made possible in part by the following grand patrons, who preordered the book on Inkshares. com. Thank you.

Bill & Debbie Giudice
Bobbie Barnett
Charles "CB" Lorch
Dale and Merle Barnett
David D. Redfield
Eileen Sullivan Mijares
Eric Abrahamsen
Eugenia L. Coyne
Gerry Littlefield
Glenn Sharron
Heather S. Ashley

Holly Lofland
Janet Hinkle
Jim G. Bettinger
Kathleen Laufenberg
    & Kent Spriggs
Kathryn P. Mitchell
Kelly S. Dozier
Kirsten Svela
Larry Levitsky
Lauren P. Milligan
Luke Edward Murphy

Margaret A. Volz
Mark Elliott
Mark Moore
Martha W. Rush
Matt Brown
Missy Bryan
Patricia J. Malarney
Richard J. Gardner
Richard Moore
Robin Lee
Roscoe Mitchell
Sam Childers
Stephanie Perkins
Tallahassee Memorial
    HealthCare
    Foundation
Tom Bevis

INKSHARES

Inkshares is a crowdfunded book publisher. We democratize publishing by having readers select the books we publish—we edit, design, print, distribute, and market any book that meets a preorder threshold.

Interested in making a book idea come to life? Visit Inkshares.com to find new book projects or to start your own.